HOW TO MAKE
GREAT STUFF
TO WEAR

. . . .

written and illustrated by

Mary Wallace

Greey de Pencier Books

How To Make Great Stuff To Wear

Books from OWL are published by Greey de Pencier Books,
56 The Esplanade, Suite 302, Toronto, Ontario M5E 1A7

*OWL and the OWL colophon are trademarks of the Young
Naturalist Foundation. Greey de Pencier is a licensed user of
trademarks of the Young Naturalist Foundation.

This book was published with the generous support of the
Canada Council and the Ontario Arts Council.

Canadian Cataloguing in Publication Data

Wallace, Mary, 1950 –
     How to make great stuff to wear

Includes index.
ISBN 0-920775-68-3

1. Handicraft.   2. Children's clothing.   I. Title.

TT698.W25 1991   j745.5   C91-094784-8

Design & Art Direction: Julia Naimska
Photography: Eekhoff & Muir Studio

Crafts on the front cover, clockwise from upper left: Paper Beads,
Spatter Painting, Papier-mâché, Carry-All, Paper Hat, Carry-All.

Crafts on the back cover, clockwise from upper left: Hand-printing,
Painted T-shirt, Silk-Painted Scarf, Two-Seam Special.

Printed in Hong Kong

A B C D E F G

INTRODUCTION

Are you looking for ways to spruce up your wardrobe? Would you like to personalize your clothes and accessories? Then read on.
You'll discover lots of ways to add pizzazz to your stuff without having to buy a lot of special craft materials. Just gather some bits and pieces from around your home and get started.

CONTENTS

You'll find pictures of all this Great Stuff To Wear on pages 35 to 42.

JEWELRY : INTRODUCTION

- Creating your own jewelry can be fun and exciting, as well as simple and inexpensive. Most of the materials and tools can be found in your own home; others are available from hardware and hobby stores at minimal cost. Good scissors, a hole punch, and small pliers are handy tools to have.

- There are many types of glue available. White glue (also called school glue) is a good all-purpose, non-toxic adhesive. However, when you want to attach a decoration securely to a metal clasp or backing, you will need a stronger glue. There are many adhesives available at your local hardware store. Have an adult help you choose one that is safe to get on your skin and has no harmful fumes, and follow the manufacturer's directions.

- Use clear nail polish, acrylic or varnish to give your jewelry a shiny protective coating. White glue can also be applied as a coating but test it first as some brands are cloudy rather than clear when dry.

- Use any type of string, thread, yarn, ribbon or lacing to string beads and pendants. Use a simple loop knot to attach pendants. Thin wire can be used to thread beads, make bracelets, or bend into interesting shapes. Never put plain wire through your pierced ears. Use only wires that have been specially designed by a professional for this purpose.

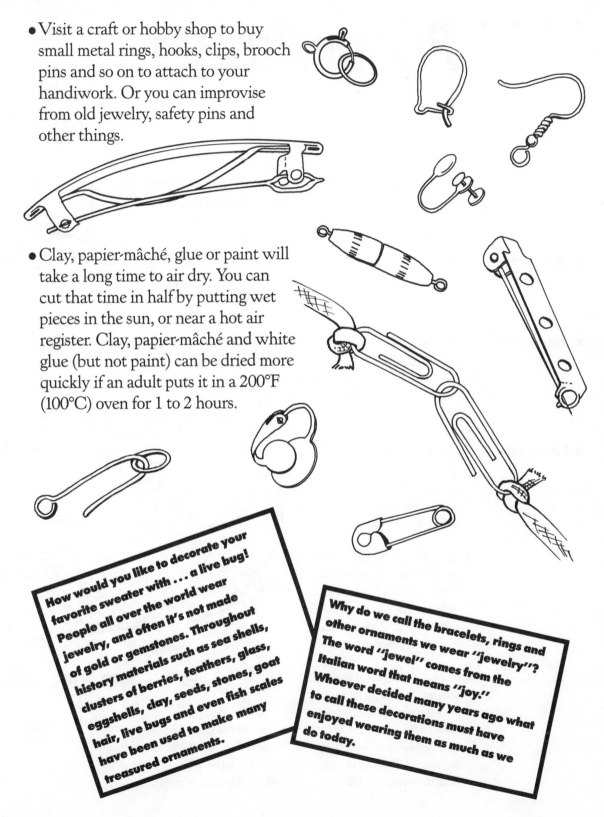

- Visit a craft or hobby shop to buy small metal rings, hooks, clips, brooch pins and so on to attach to your handiwork. Or you can improvise from old jewelry, safety pins and other things.

- Clay, papier-mâché, glue or paint will take a long time to air dry. You can cut that time in half by putting wet pieces in the sun, or near a hot air register. Clay, papier-mâché and white glue (but not paint) can be dried more quickly if an adult puts it in a 200°F (100°C) oven for 1 to 2 hours.

How would you like to decorate your favorite sweater with . . . a live bug! People all over the world wear jewelry, and often it's not made of gold or gemstones. Throughout history materials such as sea shells, clusters of berries, feathers, glass, eggshells, clay, seeds, stones, goat hair, live bugs and even fish scales have been used to make many treasured ornaments.

Why do we call the bracelets, rings and other ornaments we wear "jewelry"? The word "jewel" comes from the Italian word that means "joy." Whoever decided many years ago what to call these decorations must have enjoyed wearing them as much as we do today.

PLASTIC PIZZAZZ

Recycle plastic pop bottles by cutting, coloring and heat shaping to make see-through plastic jewelry.

● **MATERIALS**
- plastic pop bottles • scissors • aluminum foil • cookie sheet
- hole punch • indelible markers, or fine sandpaper and pencil crayons

● **PREPARATION**
- Ask an adult to preheat your oven to 225°F (110°C). Make sure there is an adult with you while you are using the oven.
- Line your cookie sheet with a layer of foil.

● **INSTRUCTIONS**

1. Cut the sides of a plastic pop bottle into squares, rectangles and other shapes. Different sizes and shapes will curl and twist in different ways.

2. Clear plastic looks good, but if you like, you can color your shapes. Decorate them with indelible markers or sand the surface lightly and draw on them with pencil crayons.

3. Place your shapes on the lined cookie sheet. With an adult, bake the plastic in the preheated oven for 2 - 3 minutes. Through the oven window watch the plastic curl. Remove the tray with oven mitts and let cool.

4. Thread the beads onto string, ribbon or yarn. Some shapes may need to have holes punched in them with a hole punch.

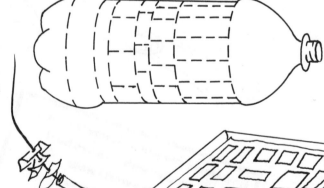

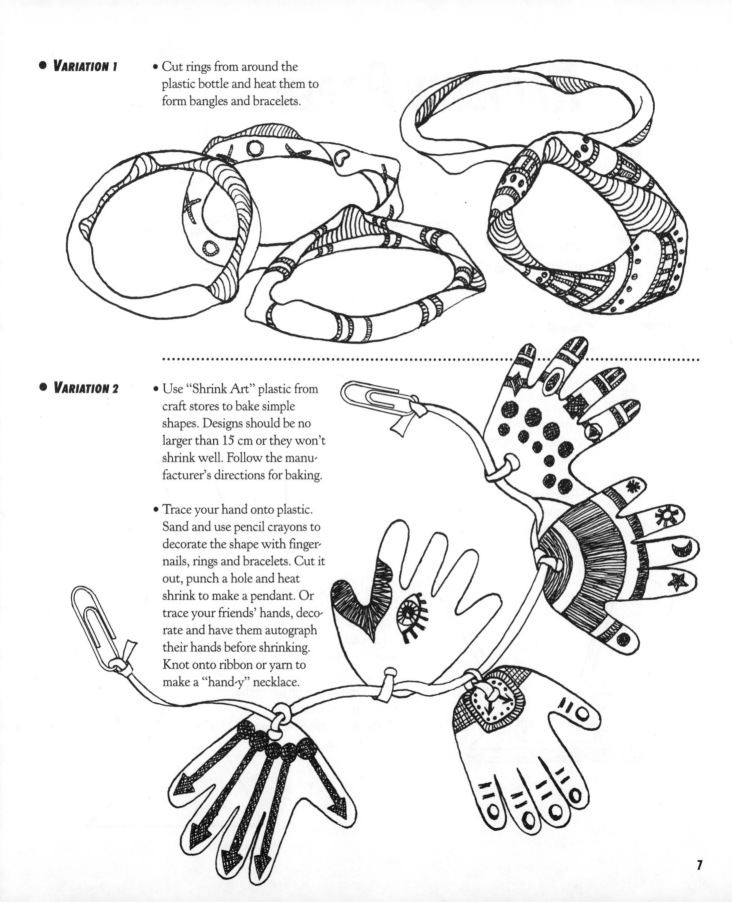

- **VARIATION 1** • Cut rings from around the plastic bottle and heat them to form bangles and bracelets.

- **VARIATION 2** • Use "Shrink Art" plastic from craft stores to bake simple shapes. Designs should be no larger than 15 cm or they won't shrink well. Follow the manufacturer's directions for baking.

  • Trace your hand onto plastic. Sand and use pencil crayons to decorate the shape with fingernails, rings and bracelets. Cut it out, punch a hole and heat shrink to make a pendant. Or trace your friends' hands, decorate and have them autograph their hands before shrinking. Knot onto ribbon or yarn to make a "handy" necklace.

RAINBOW PAPER

Cut and glue different colors of construction paper into layers and sand the result to make bracelets, beads and pendants.

● **MATERIALS**
- several colors of construction paper • pencil • scissors • white glue • brush
- sandpaper, medium and fine

● **INSTRUCTIONS**

1. Draw a simple shape on construction paper. Diamonds, circles, squares, triangles and ovals work well.

2. Trace and cut 30 or more copies of your chosen shape from various colors of construction paper.

3. Spread white glue evenly with a brush or finger on one piece of paper and place a second piece on top, lining up the edges as evenly as possible.

4. Glue a third piece on top of this. Continue until you have glued all the shapes together, one on top of another.

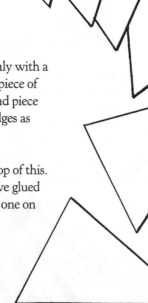

5. If you are making a pendant, carefully poke a hole through with the scissors while the glue is still wet. Once the glue has dried, it may be too hard for you to punch through.

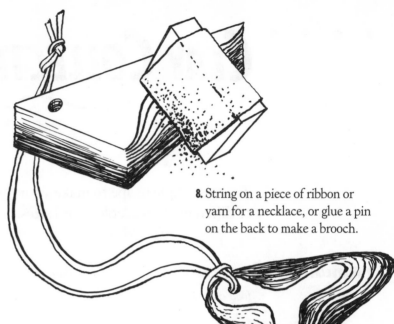

6. Let dry thoroughly, at least overnight. Sand and shape the edges with medium sandpaper. Then sand with fine sandpaper to smooth the rough surfaces.

8. String on a piece of ribbon or yarn for a necklace, or glue a pin on the back to make a brooch.

7. Give your piece a protective coating with white glue that dries clear, nail polish, clear acrylic or varnish.

• **VARIATION 1**

• To make bangles, cut and glue together rings of construction paper. Dry, sand and apply a clear finish.

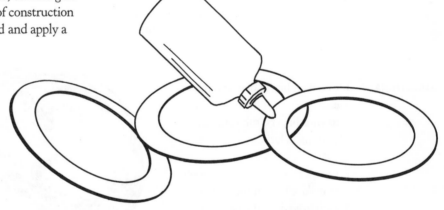

• **VARIATION 2**

• Layer and glue together a few colorful scraps of paper. Poke a hole through each. Then dry and sand to make rainbow beads.

CLAY COLLECTION

Try this simple recipe to make your own clay beads of different shapes, colors and sizes.

- **MATERIALS**
  - 250 g flour • 125 g salt • 5 mL alum • 80 to 125 mL water • bowl • waxed paper
  - food coloring (optional) • varnish, acrylic or clear nail polish (optional) • latex or acrylic paint (optional)

- **PREPARATION**
  - Combine the flour, salt and alum in a bowl. Add water, a little bit at a time, until you get a stiff ball of dough.
  - Cover your work surface with waxed paper. Knead the dough well, until it has become a uniform, non-sticky clay.
  - If you like, divide the dough into portions and add a few drops of coloring to each portion. Knead until the color is mixed through.

- **INSTRUCTIONS**

1. Pinch off bits of clay and roll each into a ball. If the clay sticks to your fingers, rub your hands with hand lotion.

2. Poke a straw or pencil through to make a hole in the middle of each bead. Dry the beads on waxed paper.

3. Glaze your beads with nail polish, clear acrylic or varnish, or paint them. To paint or glaze, rest each bead on the end of a pencil or a straw cut to a point and stuck into a lump of clay or plasticine.

4. String your beads together into a necklace or bracelet.

5. Wrap up any unused clay well and store it in the refrigerator.

- **VARIATION 1**
  - For different bead shapes, make clay cylinders, squares and ovals. Make beads in the shape of vegetables, fruits or animals. Or coil the clay around a straw to make a spiral bead. Press the outside of any bead with a fork to add texture.

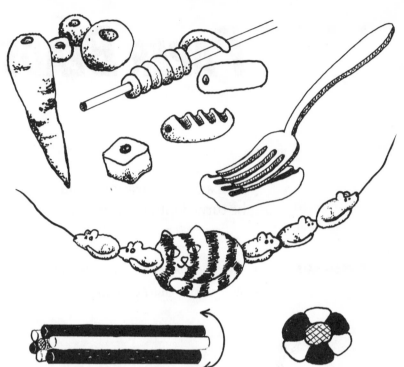

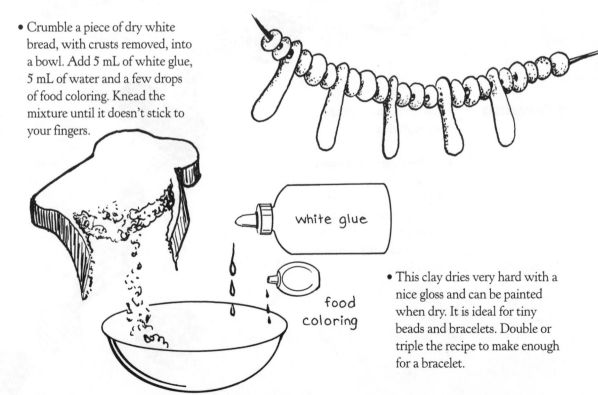

  - Add spots and coils of different-colored clay. Wet the end of the clay to be added so it will stick to the bead.

  - Roll different colors together and slice for patterned beads.

roll and slice

- **VARIATION 2**
  - Crumble a piece of dry white bread, with crusts removed, into a bowl. Add 5 mL of white glue, 5 mL of water and a few drops of food coloring. Knead the mixture until it doesn't stick to your fingers.

white glue

food coloring

  - This clay dries very hard with a nice gloss and can be painted when dry. It is ideal for tiny beads and bracelets. Double or triple the recipe to make enough for a bracelet.

PAPER BEADS

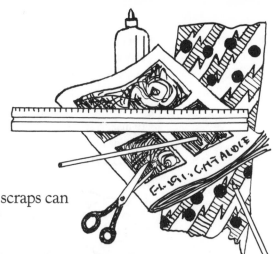

Strips of old magazines, comics and other scraps can be turned into jazzy beads.

● **MATERIALS** ● *magazines, comics, gift wrap, other paper scraps* ● *ruler* ● *pencil* ● *scissors* ● *drinking straws*
● *glue* ● *nail polish (optional)*

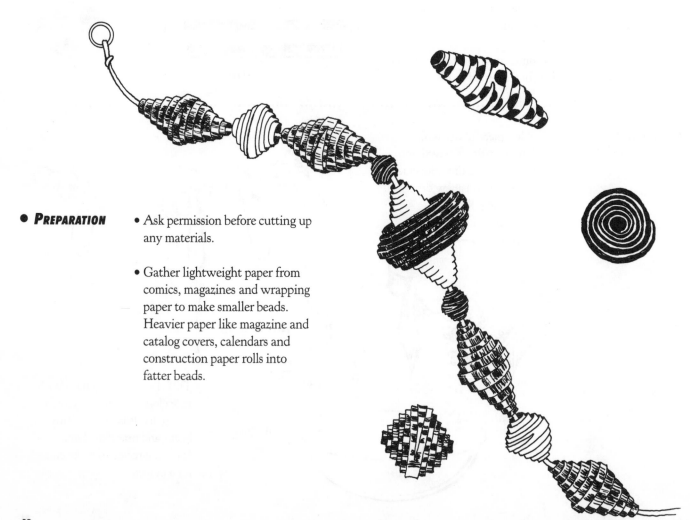

● **PREPARATION** ● Ask permission before cutting up any materials.

● Gather lightweight paper from comics, magazines and wrapping paper to make smaller beads. Heavier paper like magazine and catalog covers, calendars and construction paper rolls into fatter beads.

1. Using a ruler, draw long narrow triangles on your paper. Cut these out carefully.

2. Spread glue on the last few centimetres of the tip of one paper triangle. Starting at the widest part, roll the triangular strip around a drinking straw. The glued tip will hold the bead together.

3. For an even fatter bead, glue several long strips end to end and cut a very long triangle from them. Roll this longer triangle like the others.

4. For a clear protective finish, brush white glue onto each finished bead or coat each one with nail polish.

5. After the beads have dried, pull out the straw or snip off the ends. String your beads on some braided string, twine, shoelace or any cord that is fairly strong.

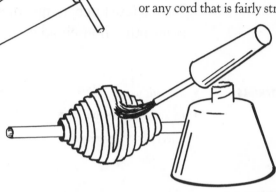

● **VARIATION**

• Roll ribbon into beads. Don't cut the ribbon into triangles. Just spread glue on the whole upper surface and roll around a straw.

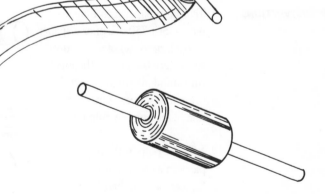

13

PAPIER-MÂCHÉ

Turn a few kitchen ingredients, newspaper and some other household items into bangles and beads.

● **MATERIALS**
- *250 mL water* • *250 mL flour* • *80 g salt* • *newspaper* • *2 bowls* • *spoon* • *pencil* • *vaseline*
- *waxed paper* • *paint* • *ribbon, yarn or string* • *cardboard tube or plastic container* • *sandpaper*
- *safety pin or brooch pin*

● **PREPARATION**
- Cover your work surface with newspapers.
- In a bowl mix up the flour, water and salt. This mixture is your basic papier-mâché paste.

BEADS

● **INSTRUCTIONS**

1. Tear newspaper into 1 cm x 1 cm pieces. Stir 750 mL of newspaper into a large bowl of water, until each piece is wet. Let the mixture stand overnight. Next day, drain and squeeze out excess water, leaving the pulp moist.

2. Mix the pulp with the basic paste in a bowl. Stir well. Squeeze a small handful of this mush around a pencil that has been greased lightly with vaseline. Work with the mush until it is a shape you like. Gently slide the bead off the pencil and place it on a piece of waxed paper to dry.

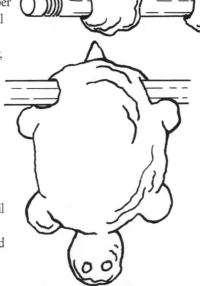

3. When dry, paint the beads. If you use tempera paint, coat the beads with shellac or varnish so the paint won't rub off. Or use latex paint or acrylic paint, which are waterproof when dry. String your beads onto ribbon, yarn or string to make a necklace.

BANGLES

● **INSTRUCTIONS**

1. Cut a ring from a cardboard tube or plastic container. Your finished bracelet will be a little wider than the ring you cut.

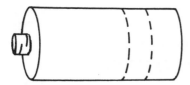

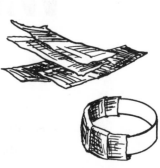

2. Tear newspaper strips about 4 cm x 20 cm. Dip one strip at a time into the basic papier-mâché paste, and pull out between two fingers to remove excess paste. Wrap this strip around the bangle form.

3. Continue dipping and wrapping strips of papier-mâché around the bangle until it is covered in three layers of strips. Smooth out any bumps or rough edges with your fingers.

4. Let dry, at least overnight. If some of your edges are too rough, smooth them by rubbing with sandpaper. Paint with several coats of paint.

FLOWER PINS

● **INSTRUCTIONS**

1. Brush the basic papier-mâché paste on between six layers of newspaper squares.

2. Cut and shape the resulting pad while it is still wet to form the petals of a flower shape. To make a double layer of petals, cut and shape a smaller pad and glue it inside the center of the larger petals with more paste.

3. Let dry thoroughly and paint.

4. Use a papier-mâché strip or tape to attach a safety pin or brooch pin onto the back.

WHITE GLUE PAPIER-MÂCHÉ

Use this to make strong, shiny, "wet look" buttons and bangles that don't require paint or any other finish.

● **MATERIALS**
- clear-drying white glue • water • bowl • brush
- paper (colored paper, brown paper, tissue paper, etc.) • cardboard

● **PREPARATION**
- Cover your work area with newspapers.
- Mix one part white glue with one part water in a bowl.

● **INSTRUCTIONS**

1. Cut forms for buttons and bangles from cardboard.

2. Apply several layers of torn paper, brushing liberally with the glue mixture as you add each piece. The glue dries clear, giving a "wet look" to the paper.

3. Bits of torn brown paper bags will look like leather. Layers of torn tissue paper will give a crinkled glass effect. Torn color comics will give a bright, crisp look. Try using wrapping paper, magazines, paper towels and so on for other looks.

- **VARIATION**

- Mix equal amounts of clear-drying white glue and water.

- Cover a jar lid with some colored tissue paper and brush the glue mixture all over it.

- Tear off small pieces of tissue paper of various colors and scrunch each one into the shape of a piece of fruit or a vegetable. Coat each shape with the glue mixture.

- Place the shapes apart from each other on a piece of plastic to dry.

- Arrange your shapes in the lid like fruit in a bowl and glue them in place. Glue a pin on the back to make a brooch.

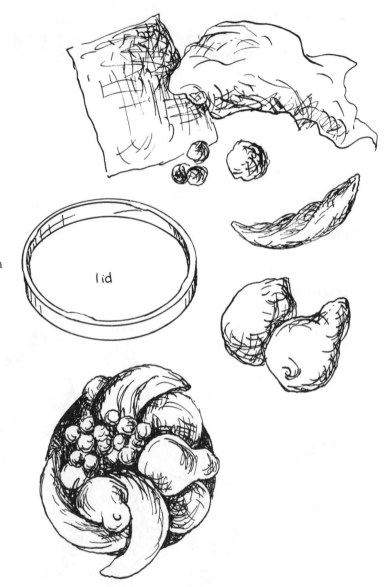

lid

ORIGAMI ART

Fold paper to make attractive lightweight jewelry.

- **MATERIALS** • *paper* • *scissors* • *ruler* • *pencil* • *earring wires* • *yarn or ribbon* • *large darning needle*

- **PREPARATION**
  - Gather as many different kinds of scrap paper as you can. You may find that some work better than others.

  - Cut each piece of paper into a square. The size of each square is up to you.

- **INSTRUCTIONS**

  1. Choose one of the designs shown. Fold your paper as accurately as you can.

  2. Make your creases crisp and neat by pressing firmly along each fold with the back of your thumbnail.

  3. Poke a hole in each folded shape and attach to yarn or ribbon to make a necklace, or fasten them onto special earring wires. Never put anything other than special earring wires from a store in your pierced ears.

FISH

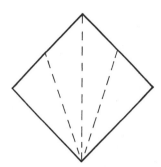 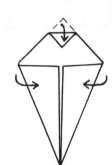  

FAN

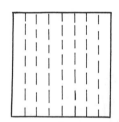 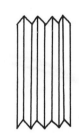 

PAPER AIRPLANE

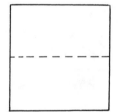 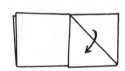 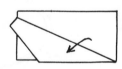 

BIRD

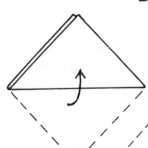 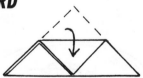 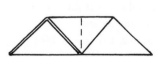

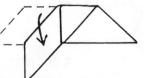 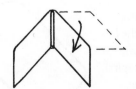

CRAZY YARN CIRCLES

Use white glue and yarn to make colorful pendants.
You will need a lid from a juice can that opens with
a plastic pull-strip.

● **MATERIALS**
- *juice can lid with rimmed edge* • *newspaper* • *hammer* • *nail* • *white glue* • *yarn* • *scissors*
- *ribbon or brooch pin*

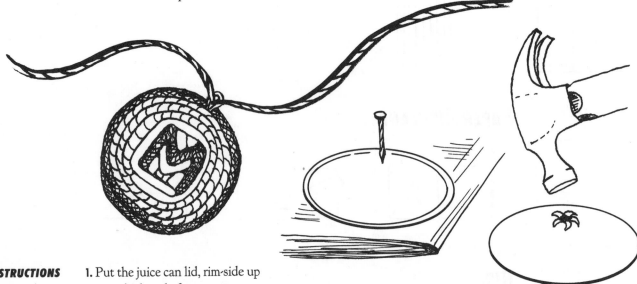

● **INSTRUCTIONS**

1. Put the juice can lid, rim-side up on a thick pad of newspaper. Carefully punch a hole near the top edge using a hammer and nail. Use the hammer to bang down the rough edges around the hole on the back.

2. Spread a thick layer of glue on the front in the center of the lid. Beginning in the center, wind the yarn around in a tight spiral. Press it down into the glue.

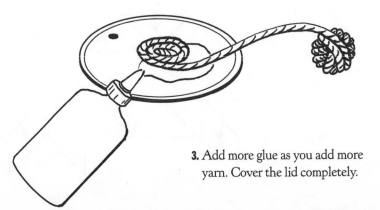

3. Add more glue as you add more yarn. Cover the lid completely.

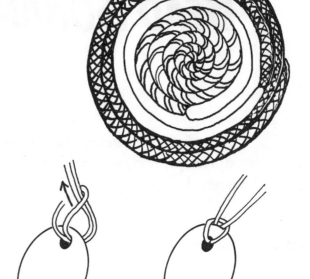

4. Change colors of yarn if you like. Snip the yarn where you want your first color to end. Butt the next color up to the last and continue.

5. Make a loop knot through the hole to attach your pendant to a ribbon as a necklace. Attach several yarn circles or add tassels and pompons. Or glue a brooch pin to the back.

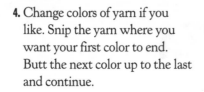

● **VARIATION 1**

● Instead of using a juice can lid, glue your yarn pattern directly to a sheet of cardboard. Trim the edges off after the glue has dried.

● Fill in spaces around an initial or other odd shape with small cut pieces of yarn.

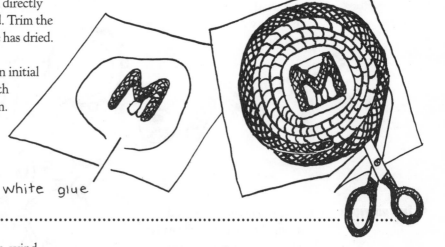

white glue

● **VARIATION 2**

● To make a wrist bangle, wind yarn around a cardboard or plastic ring. Use lots of white glue.

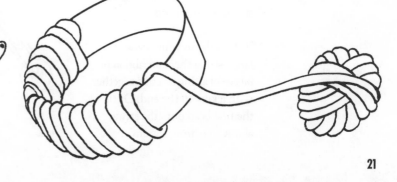

21

BEAD BONANZA

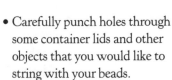

Take apart old jewelry, add sequins, new beads, straws, paper clips, seeds and other objects to create a new look.

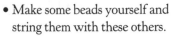

- **MATERIALS**
  - beads • other small objects • needle or smaller beading needle • strong thread

- **PREPARATION**
  - Look through your cupboards and drawers to come up with things to thread. Straws, safety pins, washers, paper clips, almost anything with a hole through it will work.

  - Carefully punch holes through some container lids and other objects that you would like to string with your beads.

  - Make some beads yourself and string them with these others.

- **INSTRUCTIONS**
  1. Thread a needle with good strong thread. For small beads tie a large knot about 3 cm from the end of the thread and begin stringing your beads.

  2. If the holes in your beads are large, string them on ribbon or pieces of string braided together with a knot in the end. Or tie the first bead onto the string about 3 cm from the end.

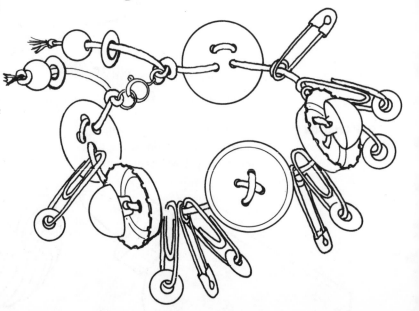

3. When you have strung as many beads as you want, tie the two ends of the thread together with a strong knot.

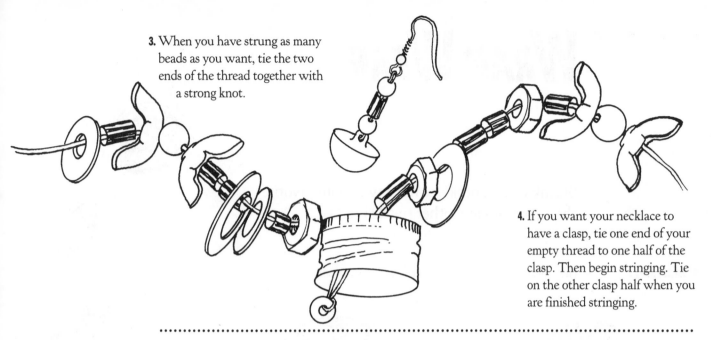

4. If you want your necklace to have a clasp, tie one end of your empty thread to one half of the clasp. Then begin stringing. Tie on the other clasp half when you are finished stringing.

● **VARIATION 1**

• Soak sunflower or pumpkin seeds in water for an hour to make them easier to thread. Carefully use a hammer and nail with a block of wood to punch holes through acorns, chestnuts and other natural beads. Alternate these "beads" to make a natural necklace.

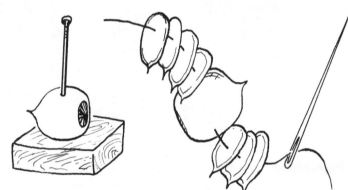

● **VARIATION 2**

• Create other designs by re-threading back through some beads as shown.

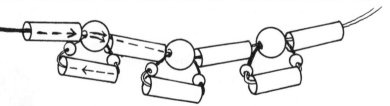

● **VARIATION 3**

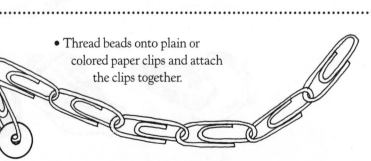

• Thread beads onto plain or colored paper clips and attach the clips together.

WRAP WEAR

Shrink wrap a necklace filled with your favorite shells, pebbles and other small objects.

- **MATERIALS** • *clear plastic wrap* • *pebbles, shells and so on* • *aluminum foil* • *cookie sheet*

- **PREPARATION**
  - Have an adult preheat the oven to 225°F (110°C). When you are ready to use the oven, ask for an adult's assistance.

  - Find some small objects that you would like to have in your necklace.

  - Cover the cookie sheet in a layer of aluminum foil.

24

• INSTRUCTIONS

1. Cut a piece of plastic wrap that is as long as you want your necklace to be. It should be long enough to go over your head.

2. Space your small objects evenly along one edge. Don't use too many objects or your necklace may become too heavy to wear.

3. Roll up the objects in the plastic wrap until there are two layers of plastic around them. Trim off the excess plastic.

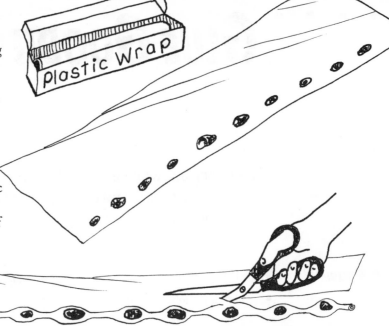

4. Twist the plastic wrap between the objects and tie the ends together.

5. Place your necklace on the cookie sheet and bake in the preheated oven for two to three minutes. The plastic should shrink just enough to hug the wrapped objects.

6. Remove from the oven and cool.

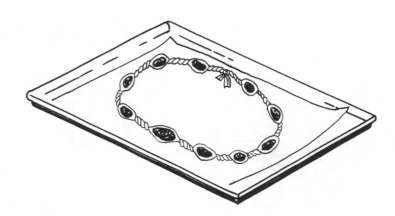

• VARIATION

• Cut a photo to fit snugly inside a jar lid. Fold a piece of plastic wrap around it so the ends meet at the top.

• Twist the plastic ends together until the wrap stretches tightly around the lid. Tie the plastic end around the arm of a safety pin and trim with scissors.

GLUE GOODIES

Blobs of plain white glue can be turned into brooches, bracelets and earrings with the help of a little hot water.

• *white glue* • *waxed paper* • *scissors* • *hot tap water* • *bowl* • *food coloring (optional)* • *toothpick (optional)*

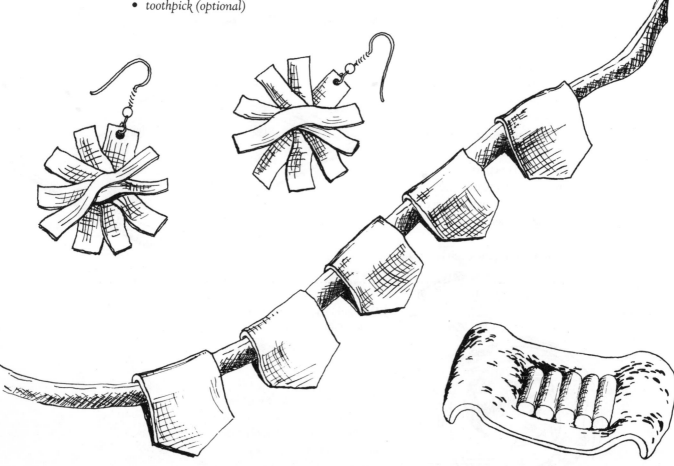

- **INSTRUCTIONS**

1. Squeeze out a pool of white glue onto waxed paper. For colored blobs, mix in a few drops of food coloring with a toothpick. Let the blobs dry completely, at least overnight.

2. When the blobs are dry, ask an adult to fill a bowl with tap water that is hot, but not hot enough to burn you.

3. Peel a dried blob off the wax paper and dip it into the hot water to make it soft and pliable. Cut it with scissors, roll, bend or twist it into any shape you like.

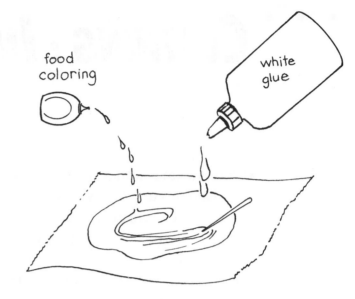

food coloring

white glue

4. Attach pieces simply by pressing them together. If the pieces become too stiff and dry, dip them into hot water again.

5. Place the shapes on waxed paper and let them dry thoroughly. Punch holes in them to make pendants or glue on brooch pins when the shapes are dry.

- **VARIATION**

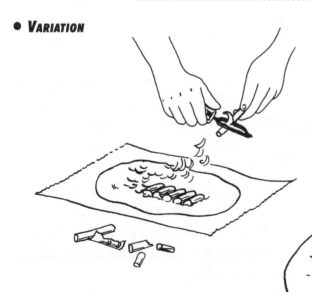

- Use a vegetable peeler to scrape bits of colored wax from crayons. When you are squeezing out new blobs, sprinkle the crayon bits onto the glue or push small broken crayons into the blob. Let dry, trim with scissors, then dip in hot water and shape. Dry again before punching holes or attaching pins.

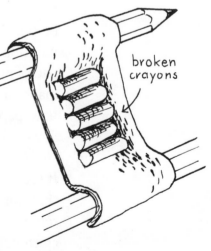

broken crayons

brooch or hair clip

CLOTHING : INTRODUCTION

- One-of-a-kind clothes are fun to make and fabulous to wear. Almost anyone of any age can create their own designer clothing. Rejuvenate old T-shirts, shirts, sweats, socks, pants and skirts. Be sure to ask an adult for help or permission before you begin, especially if you want to use old clothes or material.

- If you are painting new clothing, prewash and dry it first so the paint will soak in better. Prepare your clothing for painting by stretching it over a pad of newspaper so that the material is fairly taut. Make small newspaper pads to fit in the sleeves. This will give you a good, firm surface so you can apply paint evenly. It will also keep the paint from going through to the other side. Do not remove this newspaper or move the clothing until it is dry, or you may get paint on a clean spot. You can use a hair dryer to speed the drying process.

- Fabric dyes and paints are available in most craft, hobby and fabric stores. They come in wonderful colors and textures: fluorescent or fuzzy, shiny or slick, glittery or gold. Ordinary latex housepaint may be used as well. It comes in many bright colors and is much less expensive than buying large amounts of fabric paint. Check the manufacturer's label to make sure it is non-toxic. Never use oil-based paints.

- Put paints in plastic squeeze bottles to paint lines. Or use them with a brush to paint directly on your clothing. Dilute them with water for a more watery dye.

- Never put paint, brushes or painted fabric in your mouth.

- Be sure to cover your work area with newspaper and wear old clothes, or cover up with a paint shirt, since fabric dyes and paints are difficult to remove, even when wet.

- Some dyes and paints require heat to set them. Follow manufacturer's directions. When in doubt, you can toss the dry clothing in a hot clothes dryer for 10 minutes. This is usually enough to set the dyes into the cloth. Or cover the dry, painted clothing with a cloth and have an adult press it slowly with a hot iron for five minutes.

- Wash your new clothing separately the first time. Some dyes and paints may run. Wash in cold water to keep colors bright longer.

- Just follow common sense and safety rules, and you can relax and enjoy creating your one-of-a-kind designer wardrobe.

Try to imagine what your clothes would be like without any buttons. Almost 800 years ago people fastened their loose, flowing garments with only belts and pins. Buttons were around but they were used just as decorations. Then when form-fitting clothes became popular, some clever person came up with a new use for the button. Pockets are a more recent invention. They weren't around until about 500 years ago.

Color has always been used to decorate clothing. But before artificial dyes were created, coloring clothes was a lot of hard work. Imagine having to pick hundreds of tiny scaly bugs off of cactus plants, then roasting and crushing them to a fine powder just to make a bit of red dye. Poor bugs!

Take a look at your blue jeans. That dark blue has always been a popular color. Originally the dye came from the tropical indigo shrub. Early blue-jean manufacturers weren't the first ones to produce it, however. That same dye was used in ancient Egypt, India and Rome.

SWEATSUIT FASHION

Cut, fold, twist and tie old sweats into new fashions. Sweatsuits and T-shirts are ideal for restyling because they are doubleknits which do not unravel when they are cut.

● **MATERIALS**   ● *old sweatshirts, sweatpants, T-shirts or any doubleknit fabric* ● *scissors* ● *chalk*

● **PREPARATION**

● Always get permission from an adult before cutting up any clothing.

● Use clothing that you have outgrown, or that is stretched out of shape or stained; you can cut away these parts.

● **INSTRUCTIONS**

1. Here are some ideas for cutting new fashions from old clothing. Plan your lines before you cut. Cut a pattern from paper and pin it on; or lightly draw the lines on the material with chalk, which you can rub off later.

2. Ask an adult to help you find sturdy, sharp scissors. They make it easier to cut clean lines.

3. Save cutaway parts and use them later for pouches, headbands, ponytail holders and so on.

ponytail holder

sweatshirt

halter top

sweatshirt

skirt

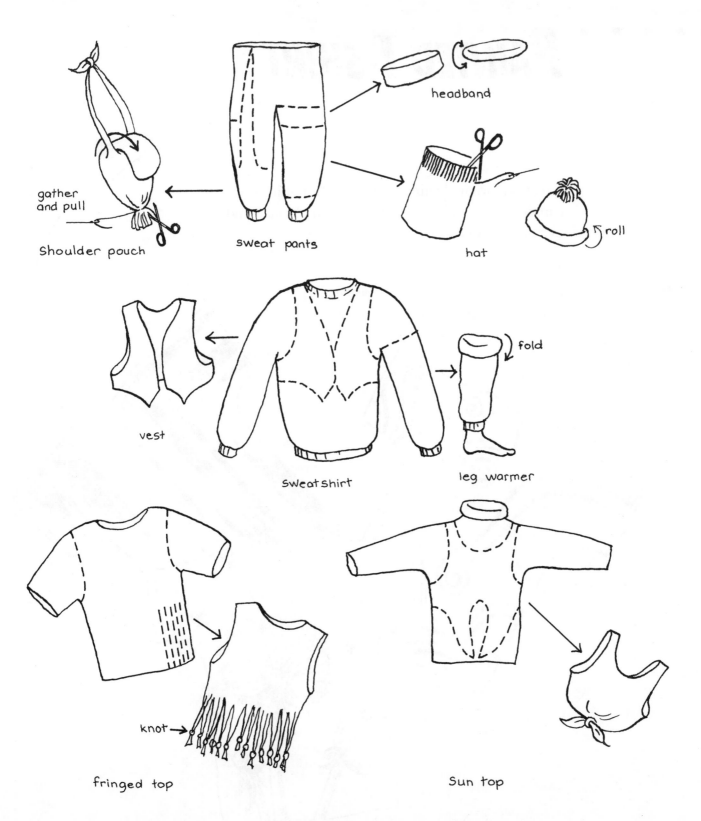

gather
and pull

Shoulder pouch

headband

sweat pants

hat

roll

vest

Sweatshirt

fold

leg warmer

knot →

fringed top

Sun top

31

PAINTED T-SHIRT

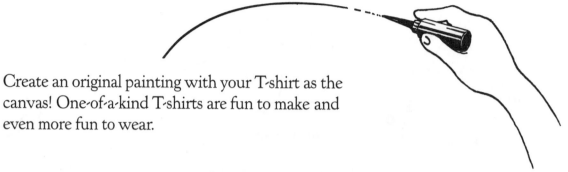

Create an original painting with your T-shirt as the canvas! One-of-a-kind T-shirts are fun to make and even more fun to wear.

● **MATERIALS**
- prewashed T-shirt ● newspaper ● paintbrush or plastic squeeze bottles
- fabric paint or latex paint ● chalk or pencil

● PREPARATION

- Pull your T-shirt over a pad of newspaper and cover the surrounding work surface with newspaper.

- Have a container of water ready so you can clean your brush between colors.

- Yellow, red and blue are primary colors. Use them to mix any secondary colors you would like (purple, green, orange, etc.). Add white to any color to make a pastel shade.

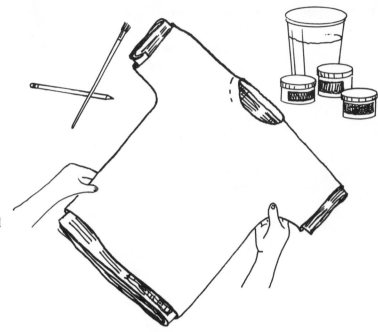

● INSTRUCTIONS

1. Lightly sketch your design on the T-shirt with chalk or pencil. These lines will wash out. Many paints stiffen when dry, so leave lots of unpainted spaces.

2. Use your paintbrush or squeeze bottle to create anything from a simple picture to an elaborate cartoon to a design with dots, squiggles and lines.

3. Choose light or bright colors for a dark T-shirt, and dark or bright colors for a light T-shirt. Contrast is the key to a snazzy shirt.

4. Don't move your shirt or take the newspaper out until it's dry. The paint might bleed into a clean spot. You can use a hair dryer to speed up the drying process.

5. Some paints require heat to set them. Follow manufacturer's directions. When in doubt, heat in a hot dryer for 10 minutes.

6. Wash your T-shirt separately the first time in case the paint or dye isn't colorfast.

- **VARIATION**

- Draw on a white or light-colored T-shirt with fabric markers, fabric crayons, ordinary wax crayons, or ballpoint pen.

- To set the fabric crayons or wax crayons, ask an adult to cover the design with waxed paper and press with a hot iron for several minutes. Fabric crayons will make a brighter design than ordinary ones.

- To set the fabric markers or ballpoint pen, put your T-shirt in the dryer on hot setting for about 10 minutes.

waxed paper

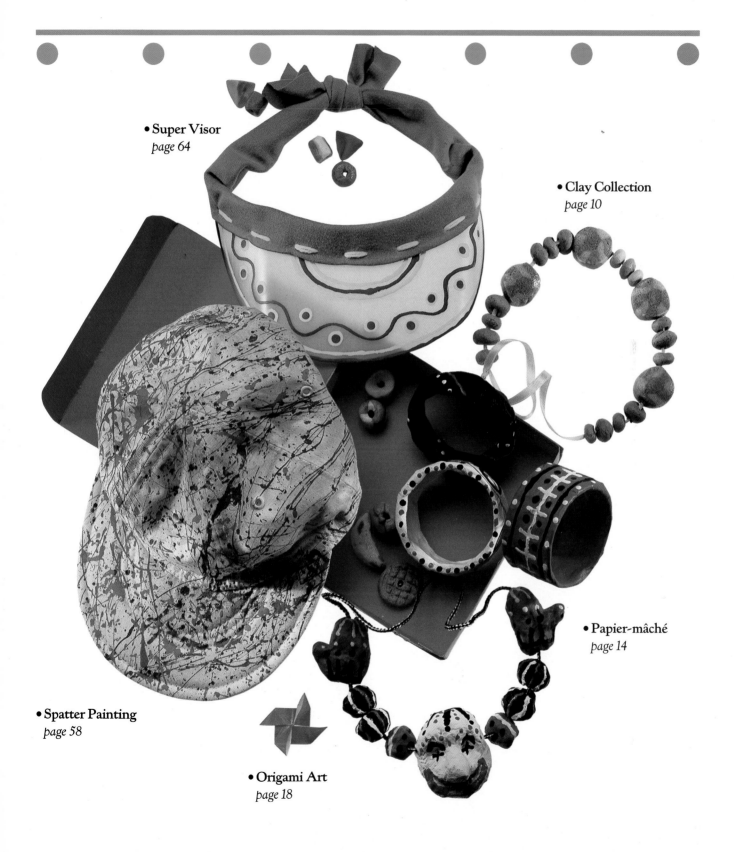

SPATTER
SHIRT

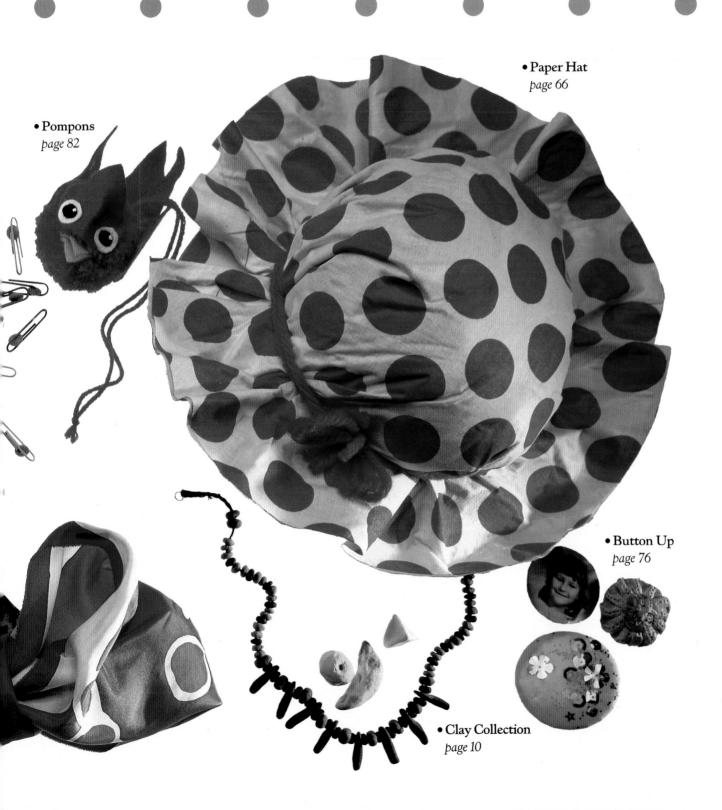

• **Paper Hat**
page 66

• **Pompons**
page 82

• **Button Up**
page 76

• **Clay Collection**
page 10

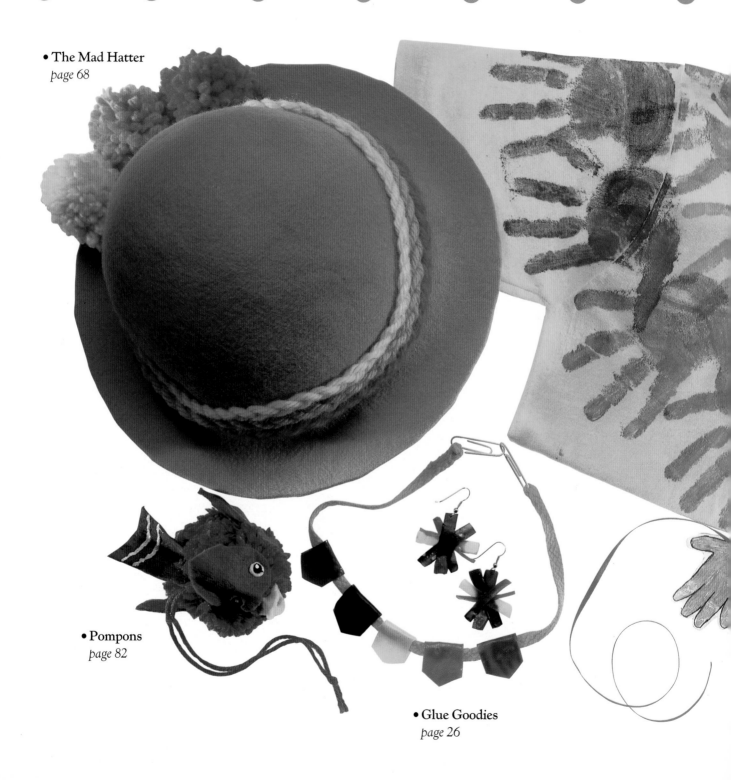

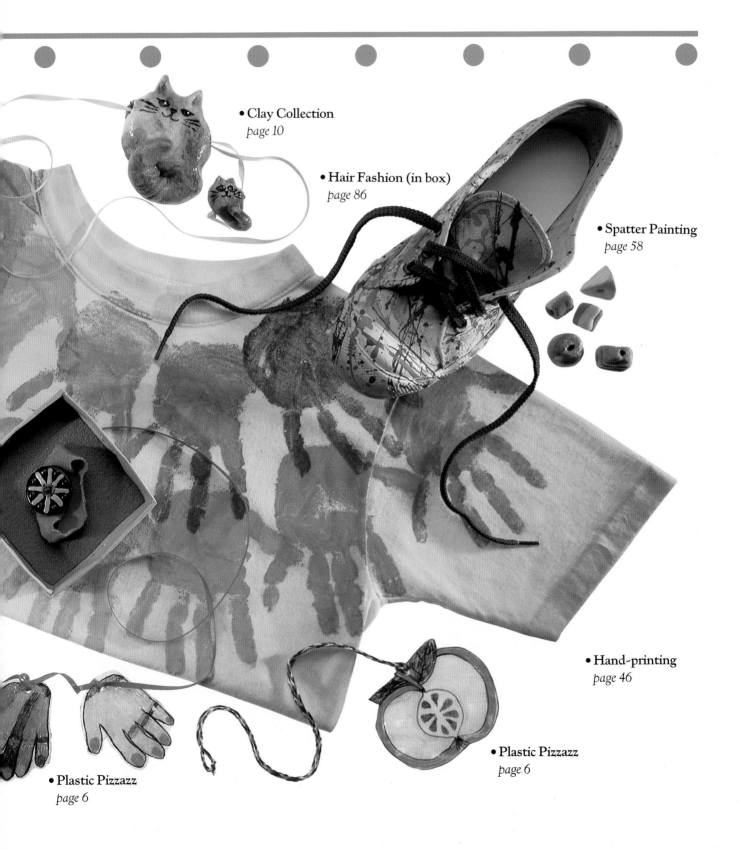

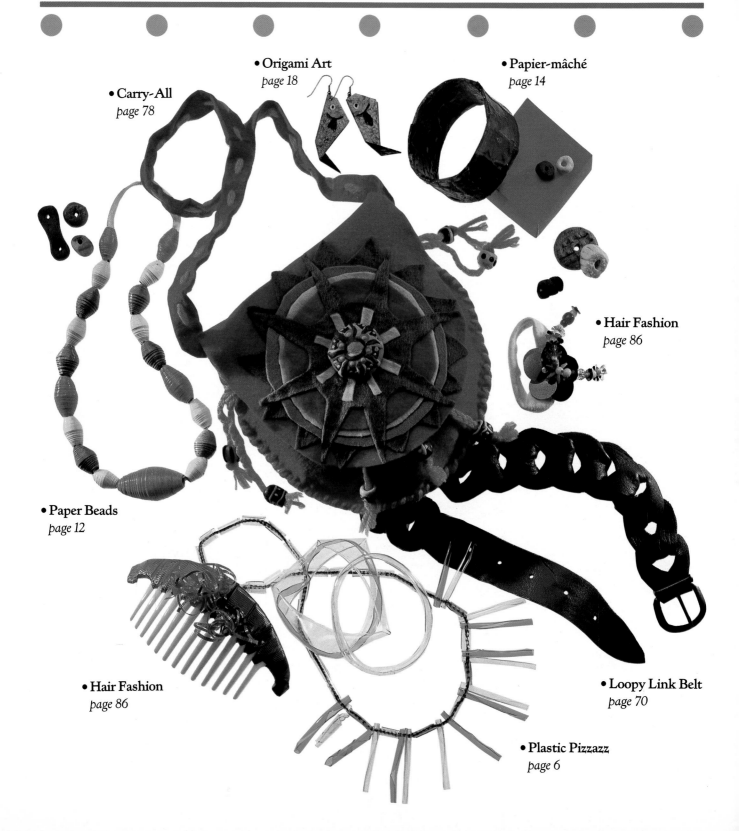

• Origami Art
page 18

• Papier-mâché
page 14

• Carry-All
page 78

• Hair Fashion
page 86

• Paper Beads
page 12

• Hair Fashion
page 86

• Loopy Link Belt
page 70

• Plastic Pizzazz
page 6

TWO-SEAM SPECIAL

This is one of the earliest and simplest patterns ever designed. Make a shirt from one rectangle of material by sewing only two short seams.

● **MATERIALS**
- *newsprint* • *pencil* • *tape* • *scissors* • *needle and strong thread or yarn*
- *large rectangle of non-fray material (felt or part of an old blanket)*

● **PREPARATION**
- Tape together sheets of newsprint to make a rectangle which is more than twice as wide as you are, and at least as long as from your waist to the top of your head.

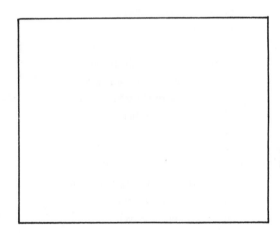

● **INSTRUCTIONS**
1. Fold down the top of the paper rectangle. The fold should be about twice the width of your arm, or a little less than one third of the rectangle. These will be your sleeves.

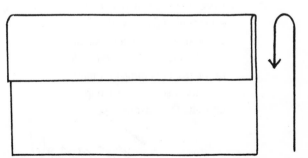

2. Measure along the top fold to find the middle. Draw an oval around that middle point for the neck opening.

3. Measure along the bottom of the pattern and mark it off in even quarters. Cut in along the bottom of the sleeve section one quarter of the way on both sides, as shown. Fold the outer quarters in to the center.

4. Cut out the neck and front openings as shown. Hold the pattern in front of you to make sure it will fit.

5. Unfold the paper pattern and place it on your material. Trace it and cut it out.

6. Thread a needle with strong, heavy thread or yarn, and knot the end. Sew the bottom edges of the sleeves together using the overcast stitch.

7. Join the middle seam with a flat joining stitch. Knot the thread at the end of each line of sewing so that it will not unravel.

8. Wear it with a belt you already have, or cut a new one from the same type of fabric as the shirt. If you like, you can add buttons. Simply sew them onto one side of the front opening. Cut matching slits or sew on yarn loops opposite the buttons.

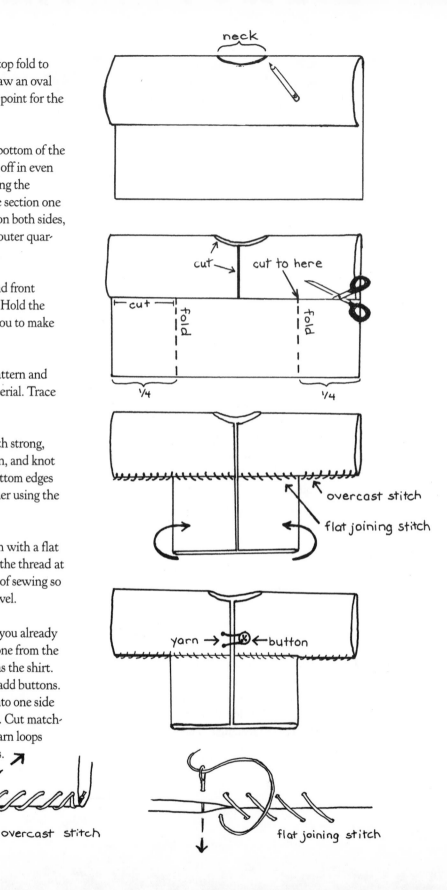

neck

cut → / cut to here

cut / fold / fold

¼ / ¼

overcast stitch

flat joining stitch

yarn → ⊗ ←button

overcast stitch

flat joining stitch

- **VARIATION 1**

- With an adult's help, you can use fusible webbing instead of thread to close the seams. Place a strip of webbing where you want the seam. Overlap the cloth pieces just enough to cover the webbing. Have an adult press with an iron. The heat through the material will fuse the seam.

- You can join each sleeve with a flat seam, or turn the front edge under for a round sleeve. For each method, pull and snip as shown.

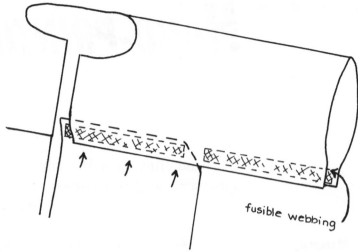

fusible webbing

or

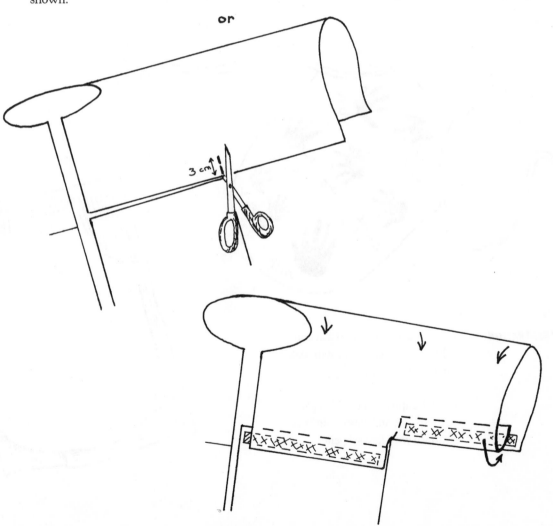

3 cm

HAND-PRINTING

Use hand-prints to make a fabulous one-of-a-kind apron for a teacher or parent.

● **MATERIALS**   • *white or light-colored apron* • *fabric paint or latex paint* • *paintbrush* • *newspaper*

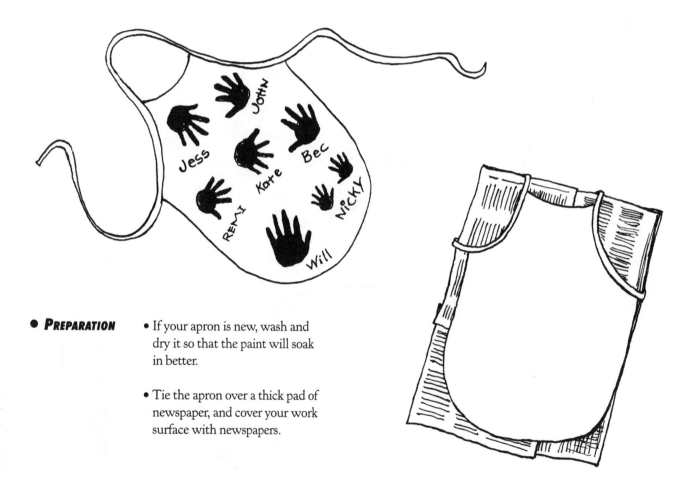

● **PREPARATION**
  • If your apron is new, wash and dry it so that the paint will soak in better.

  • Tie the apron over a thick pad of newspaper, and cover your work surface with newspapers.

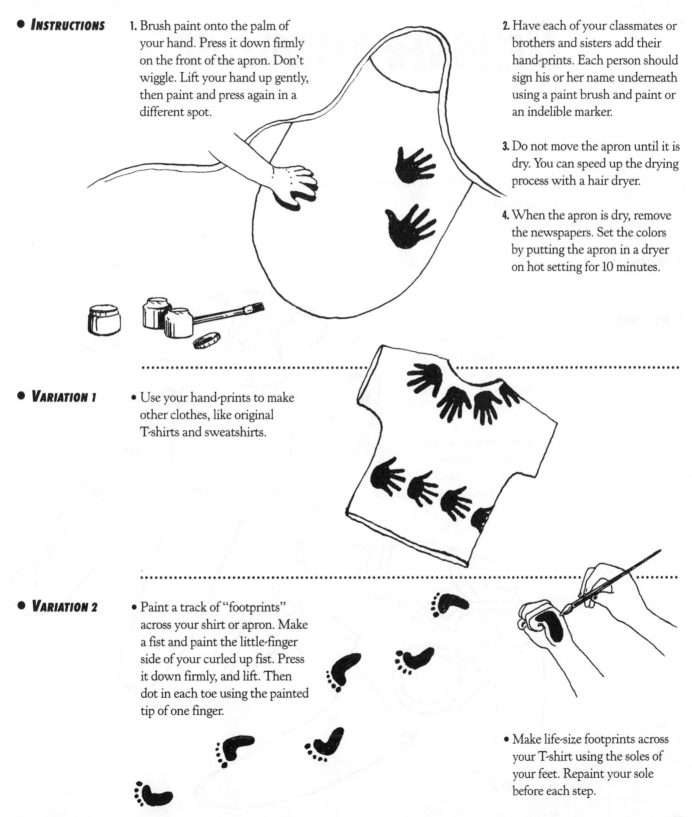

- **INSTRUCTIONS**

1. Brush paint onto the palm of your hand. Press it down firmly on the front of the apron. Don't wiggle. Lift your hand up gently, then paint and press again in a different spot.

2. Have each of your classmates or brothers and sisters add their hand-prints. Each person should sign his or her name underneath using a paint brush and paint or an indelible marker.

3. Do not move the apron until it is dry. You can speed up the drying process with a hair dryer.

4. When the apron is dry, remove the newspapers. Set the colors by putting the apron in a dryer on hot setting for 10 minutes.

- **VARIATION 1**

- Use your hand-prints to make other clothes, like original T-shirts and sweatshirts.

- **VARIATION 2**

- Paint a track of "footprints" across your shirt or apron. Make a fist and paint the little-finger side of your curled up fist. Press it down firmly, and lift. Then dot in each toe using the painted tip of one finger.

- Make life-size footprints across your T-shirt using the soles of your feet. Repaint your sole before each step.

47

• • • • DESIGNER SWEATSUIT

Design your own jazzy sweatsuit using paint and
some imagination.

● **MATERIALS**   • *prewashed sweatsuit* • *squeeze-on fabric paint or latex paint in a squeeze bottle* • *chalk or pencil*

● **PREPARATION**   • Before you begin, make sure
there is a small hole in the tip
of your paint squeeze bottle. If
there is no hole, snip off the very
tip. The bigger the hole, the
thicker the line of paint will be.

• Practise painting on a scrap of
paper. Hold the tip close to the
line to be painted and squeeze
very gently. If you get globs, you
are squeezing too hard.

48

• INSTRUCTIONS

1. Lay your sweatsuit down so it is smooth and flat. Lightly sketch your design on the front with chalk or pencil. Keep your design simple.

2. Paint the outline of your design on your sweats, starting at the top of the design and moving downward. That way you can rest your wrist and steady your drawing hand as you go.

3. Add smaller details once you've finished the outline. Fill in only small solid areas. Large painted areas become stiff and will crack when dry.

4. Leave for several hours until dry before you flip the clothes to do the other side.

5. Most of these paints don't need heat to set them. Once they have dried, the clothes are ready to wear.

6. You can wash these painted clothes in a washing machine in cold water. Hang to dry or put them in a dryer on low. Thick paint lines may stick to each other in a hot dryer. If this happens, gently pull the sweats apart and flatten them while they are still hot.

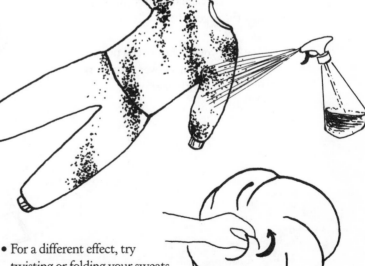

• VARIATION

• Cover your work area with newspaper. Mix one part fabric or latex paint to two or more parts water. Put the watery paint in a clean spray bottle. Hold the nozzle 5 - 20 cm from the sweats. Spray one side, then flip onto clean newspaper and spray the other side.

• If your clothes are damp when you spray them, the paints will bleed a little, giving a more muted effect.

• For a different effect, try twisting or folding your sweats before spraying.

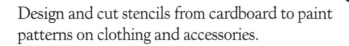

STENCILLED T-SHIRT

Design and cut stencils from cardboard to paint patterns on clothing and accessories.

● **MATERIALS**
- *paper* • *lightweight cardboard (cereal box or greeting card)* • *fabric paint or latex paint*
- *stiff paint brush* • *pre-washed T-shirt* • *newspaper*

● **PREPARATION**
- Plan a simple design on paper. This could be one shape or a combination of simple shapes, or it might be a repeating design.

- Transfer the design onto a piece of light cardboard and cut out the inside. The outside that is left is your stencil. Trim off any excess cardboard from around the edges.

- Pull your T-shirt over a news-paper pad and cover your work surface with newspaper.

- **INSTRUCTIONS**

1. Place the stencil on the T-shirt and hold it securely in place with one hand.

2. Using the brush, gently dab paint into the cutout areas. Don't overload your brush or paint may leak under the edges of the stencil. Lift the stencil carefully, move it to another spot and repeat.

3. For a pattern design, start at one edge and work across your T-shirt. Be careful not to sit any part of the cardboard down on wet paint when you stencil the next area.

- **VARIATION 1**

- Cut out different lines and shapes of masking tape and stick them onto the T-shirt. Paint around them. Let the paint dry and peel off the masking tape. Remember that large painted areas may be stiff when dry.

- **VARIATION 2**

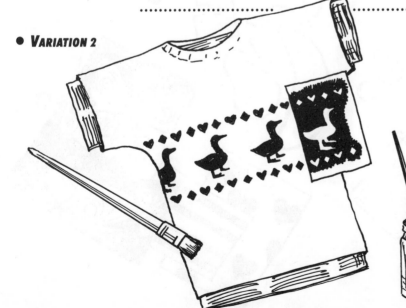

- Use the stencil method to decorate wrapping paper, binder covers, greeting cards and so on. Use tempera, latex or acrylic paints. Dab different colors into the same stencil for a more colorful effect.

PLAYFUL PATCHES

Use these eye-catching patches to cover up holes in your jeans, shorts, sweats and shirts. Or add patches just for decoration.

● **MATERIALS**   • *paper* • *pencil* • *fabric scraps* • *fabric paint, latex paint, crayons* • *needle* • *thread*

● **PREPARATION**   • Gather various scraps of fabric. Old pockets and gloves are good to use. Patterned material makes colorful patches. Get an adult's permission to use the scraps you have found.

• You will need fairly heavy material to cover a hole, but any kind of fabric will do for a decorative patch.

● **INSTRUCTIONS**

1. Decide what shape you want your patch to be: square or round, a star or a letter. Cut the shape out of paper and trace it onto the fabric scrap. Then cut out your patch.

2. Decorate your patches using paints or crayons. Use any of the painting techniques described in the sections on T-shirt and sweatsuit painting.

3. Heat-set the decorated patches before sewing them onto your clothes.

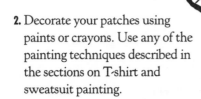

4. With a needle and thread attach the patch using a simple over-hand stitch. Hold the patch in place with straight pins or safety pins. If you place the part to be patched over a plate or book, it will be easier to sew.

5. When you have securely attached your patch to your clothing, you can add more decorations by sewing on buttons and sequins. Or you can outline the patch with squeeze-on fabric paint.

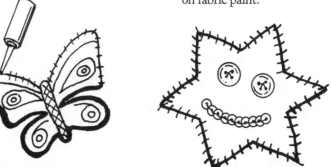

● **VARIATION 1**

• Attach patches using fabric glue. Be sure to place the part to be glued on a plate or other non-porous surface so that the glue will not stick to it if it seeps through the material.

• Ask an adult to help you attach your patches with any of the special iron-on adhesives available wherever you buy fabric.

● **VARIATION 2**

• Sew together a bunch of different patches to make a tote bag from leftover scraps.

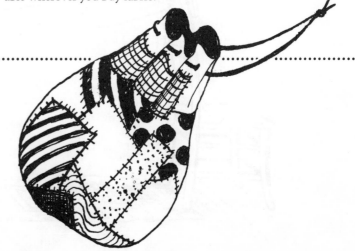

SILK-PAINTED SCARVES

"Silk painting" is the name of the technique used to paint vivid colors onto cotton, silk or synthetic fabric. With a little help from an adult, you can create beautiful scarves.

- **MATERIALS**
  - silk, cotton or polyester fabric • masking tape • straight pins • newspaper
  - old small plastic containers or lids (dye will stain) • water • washable white glue
  - liquid silk dye (that can be heat-set with an iron) • paintbrush • salt (optional)
  - needle and thread (optional)

- **PREPARATION**
  - Cut or rip your material to the size of scarf you would like. About 20 cm x 120 cm is a good size for a long scarf, and 60 cm x 60 cm for a square scarf.
  - Attach two pieces of masking tape to the backs of two chairs. Pin each of the four corners of your scarf to one piece of tape. Carefully pull the chairs apart so that the scarf is taut.
  - Cover your work area and floor with lots of newspaper, since any spilled dye may stain. Cover yourself with a paint shirt.

1. With white glue draw the outlines of your pattern on the scarf. Let dry. These glue lines stop the dye from flowing from one area to another.

2. Ask an adult to pour small amounts of concentrated dyes into the containers or lids.

3. Add water according to the directions on the bottle or jar (usually equal amounts of dye and water). Add more water for lighter colors.

4. Paint each color within the chosen area. Leave plain or, for a speckled effect, sprinkle a little salt onto the wet dye.

5. Let the scarf dry completely. If salt was used, shake it off onto the newspaper.

6. Have an adult heat-set the silk dyes by pressing with a hot iron for 10 minutes.

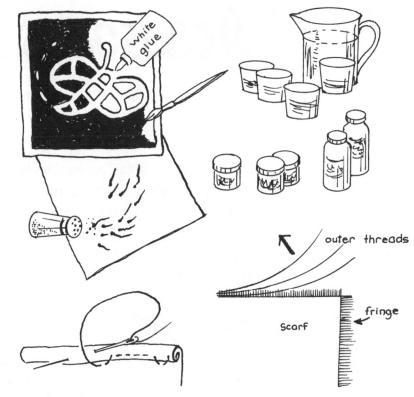

7. Soak the scarf in lukewarm water to remove the white glue and any excess dye. Rinse well. Squeeze out excess water, and have an adult iron the scarf while it is still damp.

8. To hem the scarf, roll each edge and stitch with a needle and thread. Or for a fringed finish, pull out a few threads along each edge.

● **VARIATION 1**

• Paint several colors of dye onto your scarf, letting them mix while still wet. This will give you a soft blend of colors.

● **VARIATION 2**

• Paint your whole scarf in one or more light colors. Let dry. Then paint stripes or spots on top in a different color. The wet dye will react with the dye underneath, leaving interesting "water marks."

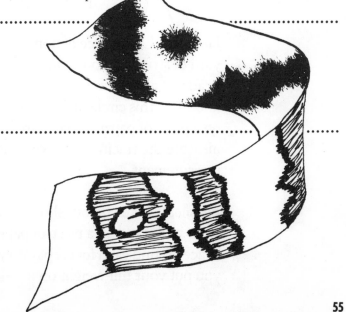

55

ACCESSORIES : INTRODUCTION

• Besides looking great, accessories have the important jobs of protecting your feet and head and holding up your pants! Hats, shoes and belts must fit well to do their jobs right. To ensure this, be sure to measure yourself properly.

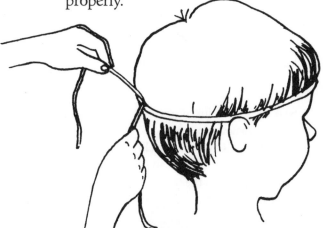

For a hat: Use a piece of non-stretch yarn or string and put it around your head just above your ears. Tie a knot. Lay this circle of string down on a piece of paper. Trace it and measure the tracing to get your head measurement.

For shoes: Take off your shoes and socks and stand on a piece of paper. Trace around each foot separately as you put your full weight on it.

For a belt: Use a tape measure or a piece of string pulled snug around your middle to get your waist measurement. Add an extra 5 cm at one end to attach the buckle. Add 20 cm to the other end so you can punch some holes to make your belt adjustable.

• Make your accessories with new materials or recycle old ones. Look through your closet and use your imagination to come up with a "new look" for old hats, belts and shoes.

• To shorten a large old belt, snip off part of the end with the holes, and add some new holes with a hole punch. Jazz up an old belt by removing the buckle and adding a new one. Decorations will add sparkle to any tired old hat. Sew or glue on buttons or patches. Wash an old pair of running shoes, add a flashy new set of shoelaces, some paint or some patches. Pompons look great on shoes, hats or belts. You can even pin hand-made jewelry onto any accessory.

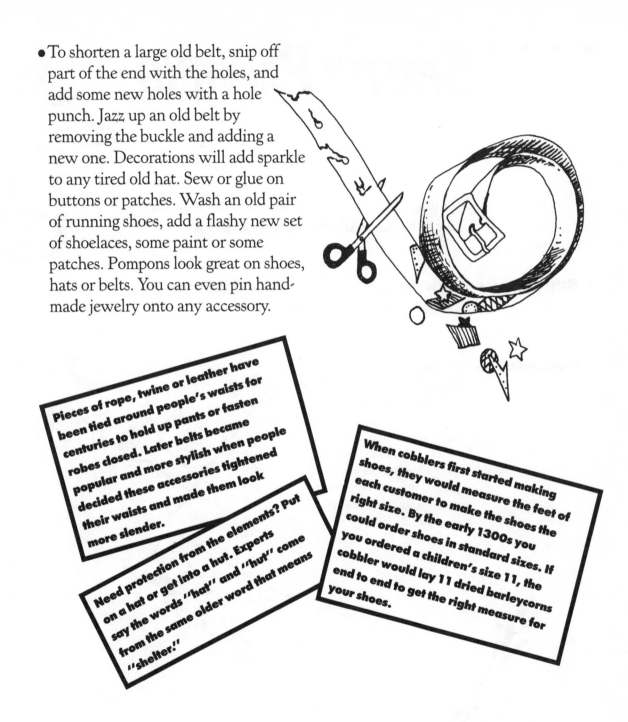

Pieces of rope, twine or leather have been tied around people's waists for centuries to hold up pants or fasten robes closed. Later belts became popular and more stylish when people decided these accessories tightened their waists and made them look more slender.

Need protection from the elements? Put on a hat or get into a hut. Experts say the words "hat" and "hut" come from the same older word that means "shelter!"

When cobblers first started making shoes, they would measure the feet of each customer to make the shoes the right size. By the early 1300s you could order shoes in standard sizes. If you ordered a children's size 11, the cobbler would lay 11 dried barleycorns end to end to get the right measure for your shoes.

SPATTER PAINTING

Sprinkle, spatter and splash an old pair of sneakers or a cap to make colorful, new accessories.

● **MATERIALS**
- old clean shoes or cap • fabric paint or latex paint • newspaper
- old toothbrush, paintbrush or whiskbroom

● **PREPARATION**
- Cover your work surface with newspapers. Cover yourself with old clothes or a paint shirt.

- Paint spattered from different brushes can look very different. Gather a few brushes of various types and sizes and experiment on newspaper to see which spatter you like best.

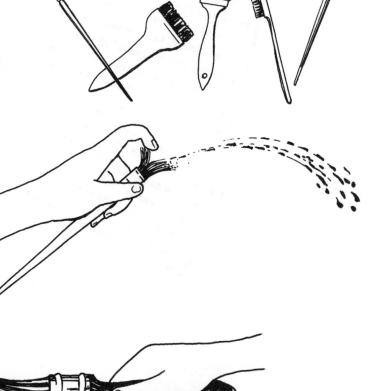

1. Dip the tip of the brush into the paint. Flick the brush, or hold the handle and run your finger across the bristles. It may take a few tries to get the knack.

2. Use one color or clean your brush and spatter with a second color. Try white spatters on dark shoes or pink and yellow on a purple cap.

3. You can spatter shoes that already have a design on them. You may want to cover the design by brushing some paint over it first.

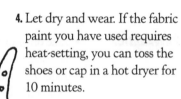

4. Let dry and wear. If the fabric paint you have used requires heat-setting, you can toss the shoes or cap in a hot dryer for 10 minutes.

• **VARIATION 1**

• You can spatter pants, bags, belts and binder covers.

• **VARIATION 2**

• Food coloring is often available in small plastic squeeze bottles. Stretch a white T-shirt over newspaper. Squirt the colors out onto the shirt drop by drop or in a nice line, depending on how hard you squeeze. When different colors overlap, they will blend, creating a rainbow.

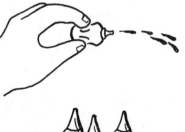

• Let dry, then put in a hot dryer for 10 minutes. Although the colors will look dark, much of the dye still isn't set. Rinse the T-shirt under cold water until the water runs clear. Then dry again. The colors will now be lovely, soft pastels. They are still not totally colorfast so remember to wash your T-shirt separately in cool water.

SLIP-ON SANDALS

Cut, fold and tie to make a pair of simple indoor sandals from a piece of foam or felt.

- **MATERIALS**
  - paper and pencil • marker or chalk • scissors • flexible foam or heavy felt • duct tape (optional)
  - white glue (optional) • hole punch • yarn or ribbon • old plastic container

- **PREPARATION**
  - Take off your shoes and socks. To make your paper pattern, trace around each foot and between your first and second toe. Then draw a second line around your footprint 3 cm out from the sides and the back and 0.5 cm out from the front.

- **INSTRUCTIONS**
  1. Fold each footprint toe to heel to find the halfway mark. Punch a hole on either side of each foot outline at the halfway mark.

  2. Punch two holes 1 cm apart between the toes, and two more holes 1 cm apart at the back of the pattern in line with the toe holes, as shown.

  3. Cut along the dotted lines.

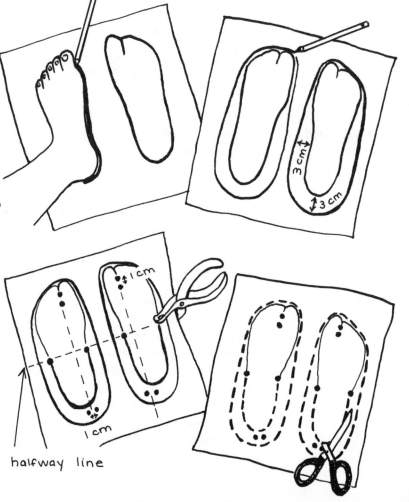

halfway line

60

4. Place your paper pattern on the foam or felt and transfer all of the lines and holes with a marker or chalk.

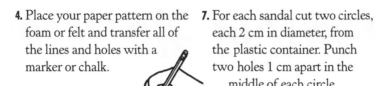

7. For each sandal cut two circles, each 2 cm in diameter, from the plastic container. Punch two holes 1 cm apart in the middle of each circle.

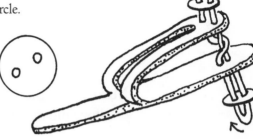

5. If you are using foam that isn't very sturdy, reinforce the bottom of the sandals with duct tape before cutting. Remove the paper pattern, cut the sandals out and punch holes through where marked.

6. If you are using felt, you will need to cut out two layers of fabric for each foot and glue them together so you have a double thickness.

8. Fold the thin strip of the sandal up from the heel to the toe. The pair of holes in the strip should be above the pair at the toe, but the holes themselves will not line up exactly.

9. Thread several strands of yarn through the circles and the sandal as shown. Pull the yarn tight but leave about 2 cm between the sole and the top strip. Tie a knot at the top and trim the ends.

fold up

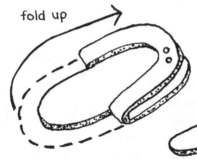

2 cm

- **VARIATION**

- From an old soft sweater cut a section of sleeve that is one-and-a-half times the length of your foot. Stitch the wide end closed.

- Into the open end insert a cardboard rectangle as long as your foot. Sew that end closed.

- Fold the wide end over and sew to the bottom section along the edges. Repeat for the other foot.

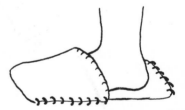

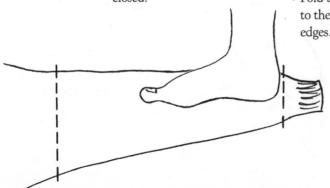

MARVELLOUS MOCCASINS

Make a two-piece pattern to cut and sew a pair of comfortable moccasins from felt or fabric.

- **MATERIALS**
  - paper and pencil • scissors • new felt or part of an old blanket • yarn and darning needle
  - beads, markers or paints to decorate

- **PREPARATION**
  - Ask permission before cutting up an old blanket.

  - Trace both of your bare feet onto paper, leaving at least 20 cm between them. Fold the foot-prints to find the halfway mark. Draw the moccasin pattern outside the outline of each foot as shown. Measure each of the distances carefully.

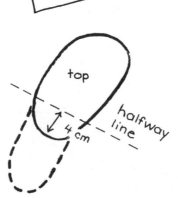

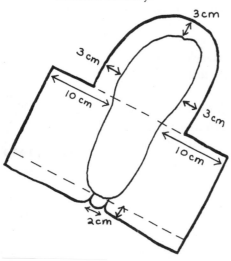

  - To make the moccasin tops, trace both feet again, fold in half and draw a line across at the halfway mark. Erase the heel half. Finish the top half with a rounded line about 4 cm past the halfway line.

● INSTRUCTIONS

1. Cut out the paper patterns and trace them onto felt. Carefully cut out the felt pieces.

2. Decorate your moccasin tops with yarn, small beads, indelible markers or fabric paints. Keep your decoration toward the toe end and at least 1 cm away from the edges.

3. Mark each top and the front half of each bottom piece into 25 fairly even sections. Begin by marking the halfway point, then the quarter points, eighth points and so on until each edge has 25 marks on it.

4. Sew the top piece to the front of each bottom as shown. Make a knot inside the moccasin at the first of your 25 marks.

5. Match each mark on the bottom to the corresponding mark on the top. Pull each stitch tight as you sew. To finish, knot the end securely in the inside.

6. Fold up the side flaps and overlap the ends at the back of the moccasin. Fold up the tab and sew in and out as shown. Knot the beginning and end of the yarn so it won't unravel.

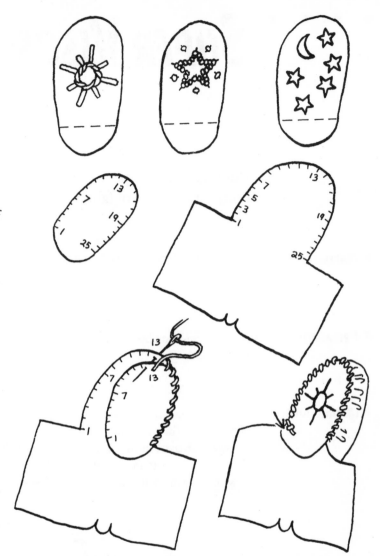

7. Fold over the side flap and top flap. Punch two holes about 3 cm apart through both thicknesses of the front flap. Tack down the bottom edge of the side flap at the front and back.

8. Pull a shoelace through the holes on the top flap and around under the side flap. Pull it snug and tie a bow.

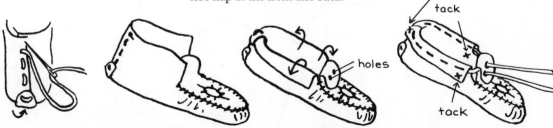

63

SUPER VISOR

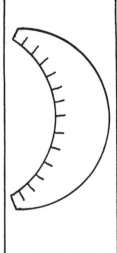

Put together a simple tie-on sun visor from a pop bottle and a scrap of fabric.

● **MATERIALS**   • *large plastic pop bottle* • *hole punch* • *scissors* • *old T-shirt or sweatshirt scrap* • *yarn and needle*

● **PREPARATION**   • Ask for permission before cutting up clothing.

● **INSTRUCTIONS**   1. Cut out and flatten the middle of the bottle. Trace and cut out the visor pattern. Punch holes as shown. Cut the slits and fold the tabs up along the dotted line.

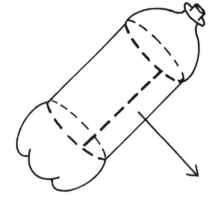

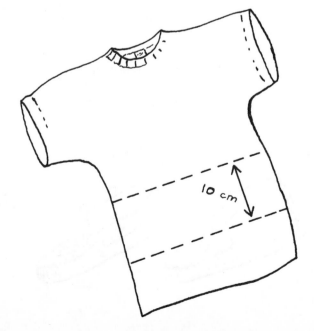

2. From the T-shirt scrap cut a strip about 10 cm wide and long enough to go around your head and tie at the back.

64

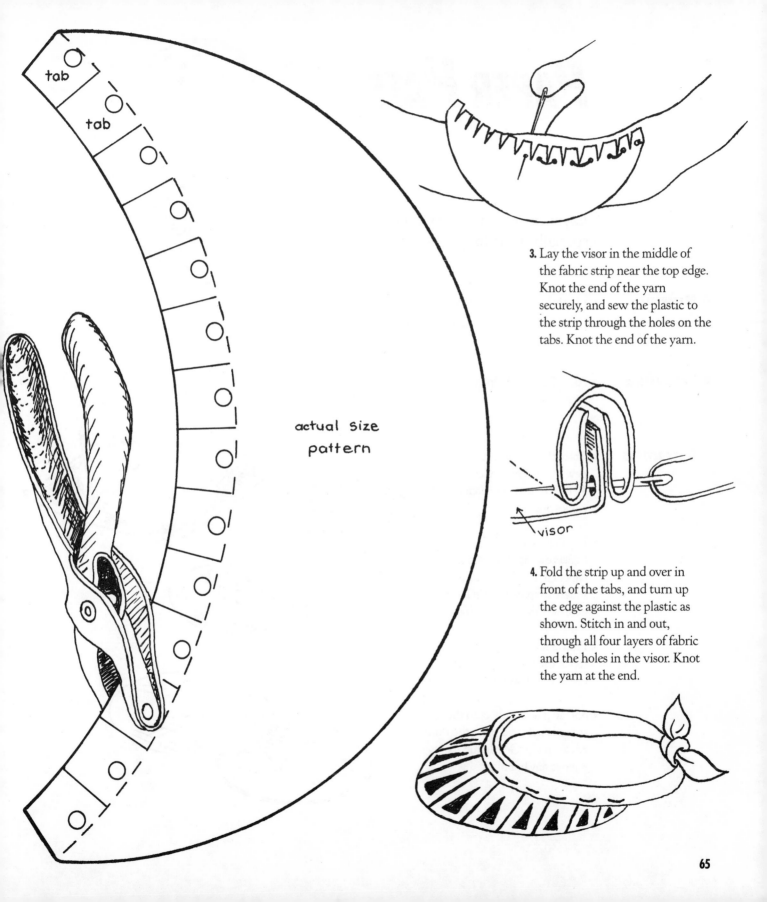

tab

tab

actual size
pattern

3. Lay the visor in the middle of the fabric strip near the top edge. Knot the end of the yarn securely, and sew the plastic to the strip through the holes on the tabs. Knot the end of the yarn.

visor

4. Fold the strip up and over in front of the tabs, and turn up the edge against the plastic as shown. Stitch in and out, through all four layers of fabric and the holes in the visor. Knot the yarn at the end.

PAPER HATS

Layer circles of newsprint together to form a hat specially made for your head.

- **MATERIALS**
  - *newsprint or newspaper* • *large circular lid (40 - 50 cm across)* • *pencil* • *scissors* • *white glue*
  - *cardboard square (5 cm x 5 cm)* • *string or yarn* • *tempera paint* • *paintbrush*

- **PREPARATION**
  - Ask a friend to help you form-fit your hat.

- **INSTRUCTIONS**

1. Trace three large circles onto newsprint. The circles should be 40 to 50 cm in diameter. Cut the circles out.

2. Lay one circle on a flat surface. Squeeze some glue onto the paper circle. Use the cardboard square to spread a thin layer of glue over the whole surface.

3. Place a second paper circle on top of the first, lining up the edges as well as you can.

4. Spread glue evenly onto this second circle and place the third circle on top. Gently rub to remove any bubbles.

5. With the help of a friend, place the circles on top of your head. Gently push down the edges to form the hat around your head.

6. Have your friend wrap a piece of string around your head and tie it.

7. Carefully lift up the edges and shape them however you like to form the brim.

8. Leave the hat on your head for 10 minutes more so that it will hold the shape. Then remove and set in the sun or near a heat register to dry.

9. When your hat is dry, trim the brim with scissors, and paint your hat. Dry your hat again before wearing it.

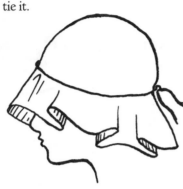

● **VARIATION 1**

● Use different types of paper for your hat. Gift wrap and color comics both work well. Or use fabric for the top and bottom layer with a layer of paper in between.

● **VARIATION 2**

● To make an extra sturdy hat, paint your dry hat with latex house paint, inside and out. Handle the hat carefully since the paint will make it soggy. When dry, the latex acts like a layer of waterproof plastic.

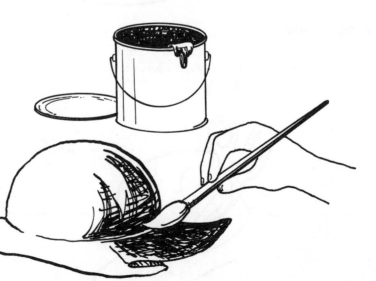

THE MAD HATTER

Change the shape of old felt hats to make new pointed, round or square hats.

- **MATERIALS**
  - old felt hat • warm soapy water • scissors • hat form (bowl, bottle, box, etc.)
  - yarn, fabric scrap or scarf (optional)

- **PREPARATION**
  - Find an old hat and get permission to recycle it. Cut off all decorations, hat bands and stitching.

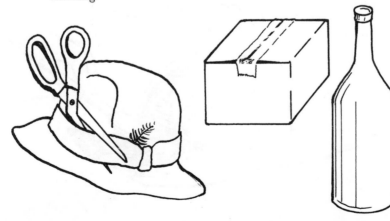

  - Set up the form on which to shape your hat. A round bowl is great for a bowler type of hat. Use a box for a square hat. A tall bottle or broom handle works well for a pointed hat.

1. Carefully wash the hat, rinse it and gently squeeze out the excess water.

2. Slowly pull and stretch the wet felt to fit the hat onto the form you have chosen. Be careful; wet felt is quite stretchy and once it is stretched out, you cannot shrink it back.

3. After forming the main part of the hat, gently pull and stretch around the bottom to form the rim slightly larger than your desired shape.

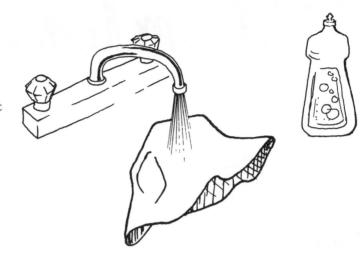

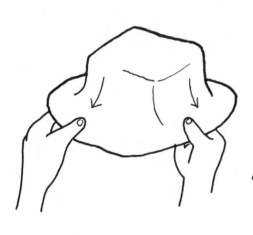

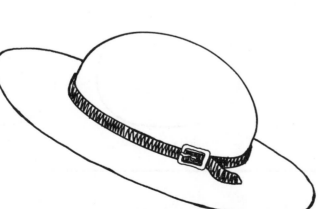

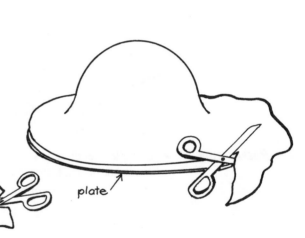

plate

4. Let the hat dry. Then trim the brim to whatever shape you like. Center the hat on a large dinner plate and use the edge of the plate as a guide for cutting a circular brim.

5. If you like, add a hat band made from a fabric scrap, braided yarn or a scarf.

LOOPY LINK BELT

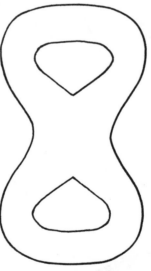

Fold leather or vinyl scraps into a super belt.

- **MATERIALS**
  - lightweight cardboard (cereal box lid) • marker or pen • scissors • leather or vinyl scraps • belt buckle • fabric or leather glue

- **PREPARATION**
  - Ask for leather or vinyl scraps from a shoe or coat factory. Or cut up a discarded coat or purse.

- **INSTRUCTIONS**
  1. Trace these pattern pieces and transfer them to cardboard. Cut them out.

  2. Trace the cardboard pattern of the buckle piece and the end piece onto the leather. Cut them out. Trace each new piece as close as possible to the one before so that no leather is wasted.

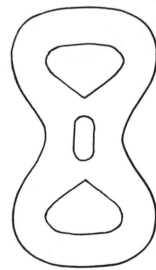

middle piece   buckle piece

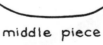

end piece (actual size)

3. Trace a few middle pieces and cut them out. Fold each link in half lengthwise to snip the triangle out of each end, cutting through both layers at once.

4. Fold the buckle piece through the buckle, with the tongue sticking through the hole in the center. Slip on a leather loop to hold the buckle snugly in place.

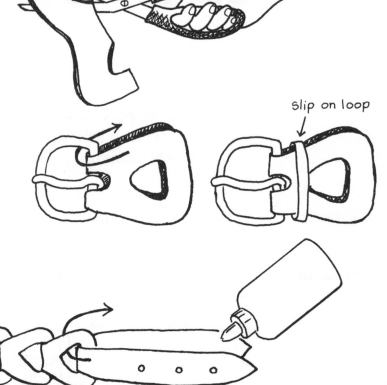

slip on loop

5. Pull a middle piece through the triangular holes in the first piece and fold it in half. Pull the next piece through the same way.

6. Continue adding belt links until the belt is long enough to go around your waist. Cut more belt links as you need them.

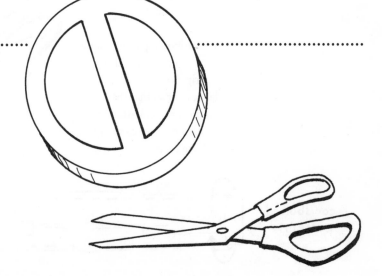

7. Pull the end piece through the last belt link and fold it in half. Glue the ends together. Punch holes for the tongue of the buckle to fit through.

• **VARIATION**

• Make your own buckle by cutting one from a plastic container lid.

SEE-THROUGH BELT

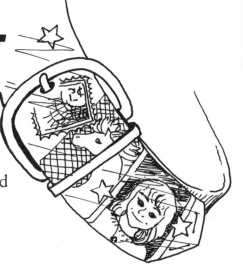

Display your favorite drawings, photos, stickers and so on in a clear plastic belt. When your favorites change, your belt can change too.

● **MATERIALS**   • *buckle* • *cardboard* • *clear tape* • *scissors* • *hole punch* • *stapler* • *clear heavy plastic*

● **PREPARATION**

• Buy a strip of clear tablecloth plastic at a hardware or department store. It can be cut to a specified width from a wide roll at the store.

• Buy a new buckle or reuse one removed from an old belt.

• Cut a cardboard pattern strip that is not quite as wide as the shank of the buckle.

shank

cardboard pattern

● **INSTRUCTIONS**

1. Cut a strip of clear plastic twice the width of the buckle shank and 20 cm longer than your waist measurement.

2. Lay the cardboard pattern along the centre of one end of the plastic strip. Fold both edges of the plastic over so that they meet in the middle. Fasten the edges with a piece of clear tape about 10 cm long.

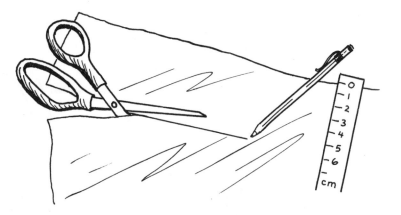

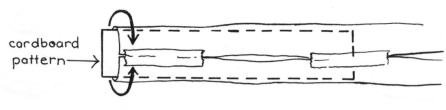

cardboard pattern →

3. Leave a space of about 10 cm and add another piece of tape. Slide the cardboard along as a guide as you continue to fold and tape.

4. Punch two holes 1 cm apart near one end of the belt. Cut out the plastic between these holes to create an oval hole.

5. Pass the belt through the buckle and slide the tongue up through the oval hole. Make sure that the taped slit is on the inside of the belt. Fold the end of the plastic belt around the buckle shank and staple it in place.

6. Finish the other end of the belt by cutting it to a point. Staple and tape the edges as shown.

7. Fold or cut cards, photos and so on to the width of your cardboard pattern. Insert these through the slit at the back of the belt so that they show through the front. Add sequins, stickers, stamps or any flat decorations.

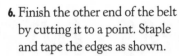

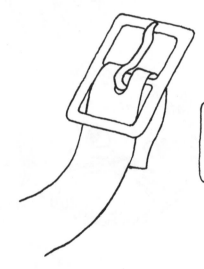

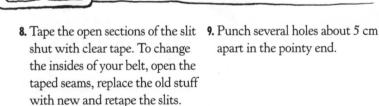

8. Tape the open sections of the slit shut with clear tape. To change the insides of your belt, open the taped seams, replace the old stuff with new and retape the slits.

9. Punch several holes about 5 cm apart in the pointy end.

● **VARIATION**

● Decorate an old belt with strips and shapes of brightly colored self-adhesive vinyl. Add details with waterproof markers or fabric paints.

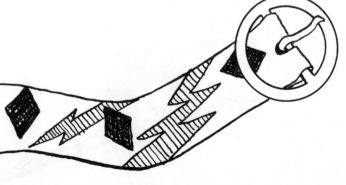

EXTRAS : INTRODUCTION

• Just as spice adds zest to food, so
extras add pizzazz to your wardrobe.
Who needs to buy the latest fads and
expensive doodads? Make great extras
by yourself or with your friends,
and have a whole lot of fun at the
same time.

• Look around you to find little odds
and ends, and use your creativity to
transform these ordinary scraps into
the unusual. Turn bits of wool into a
pompon bird or a fluffy kitty. Use
scraps of ribbon and a few beads to
make your hair accessories something
special.

• Raid the trash bin for useful materials.
Old plastic bottles can be turned into
handy lunch pails. If your orange juice
can opens with the pull of a twist tab,
save the metal lid and transform it
into a personalized button pin. Think
before you throw anything away.
Could you turn it into something else?

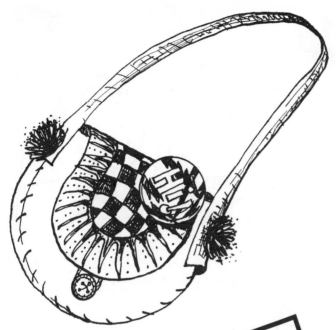

● Worn-out clothes can be useful too. Purses, pouches and backpacks can be made from heavy felt, but they can also be made from part of an old coat or heavy jacket. Even articles of clothing that are stained or badly torn can be cut up and used for these and other projects.

People have carried purses and pouches for a long time. But they didn't always hold money or house keys. In other times and cultures people have carried things that they considered valuable: amulets or charms of bone or stone, dried leaves and roots of medicinal plants, pebbles, claws and so on. Whatever the contents, these pouches and bags have always been useful.

Decorative buttons have been popular for many centuries. Some years ago in Britain it became a fad for people who were later nicknamed "Pearly Kings and Queens" to sew shiny buttons all over their clothes. One Pearly King had 13 400 gold buttons fastened to his black velvet suit.

BUTTON UP

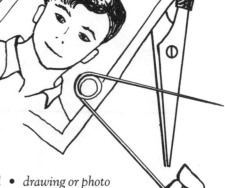

Design and create your own button pins with a photo, drawing or mini-collage. You will need a lid from a juice can that opens with a plastic pull-strip.

- **MATERIALS**
  - juice can lid • safety pin • tape • cereal box or light cardboard • drawing or photo
  - clear self-adhesive vinyl • scissors • ball-point pen

- **PREPARATION**
  - You can buy clear self-adhesive vinyl at most hardware or department stores. You will only need a small piece for each button that you want to make.

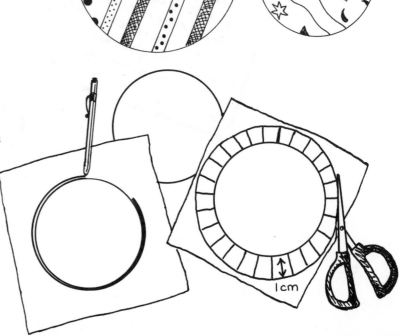

- **INSTRUCTIONS**
  1. Trace around the juice-can lid on your chosen picture and cut out the circle.

  2. Place the lid on the vinyl and trace around it with a ballpoint pen. Draw another circle 1 cm out from the first one, and connect the two circles with short straight lines, as shown. Cut out around the larger circle and snip each of the short lines.

1 cm

3. Cut a smaller circle from the cardboard, so that it will fit just inside the rim of the lid.

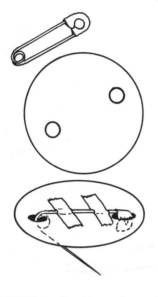

4. Put the safety pin on the center of the cardboard circle and mark the two ends. Cut a hole at each mark. Fit the pin through the holes and tape it in place.

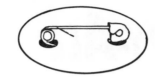

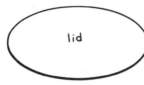
lid

photo
face down

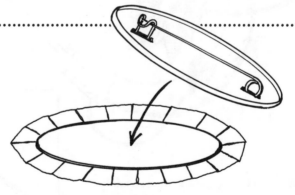
sticky side up

5. Place the cardboard circle inside the lid so that the pin opens out.

6. Peel the backing off the vinyl and carefully place your picture face down in the center. Place the juice can lid on top of the picture, with the pin-side up.

7. Carefully fold the sticky tabs, one at a time, over the edge of the lid so they stick to the cardboard. Gently rub the vinyl all over to make it stick.

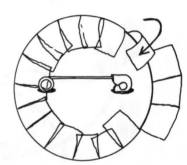

● **VARIATION 1**

• Recover an old button pin the same way. Trace a photo to the size of the button. Attach the photo to the button pin with a piece of self-adhesive vinyl.

● **VARIATION 2**

• Replace regular shirt or sweater buttons with beads. Or, decorate plain buttons with acrylic or latex paint or indelible markers.

CARRY-ALL

• • • • •

Make a backpack or purse and decorate it according to your own special style.

● **MATERIALS**
• felt, or vinyl from an old coat • paper and pencil • scissors • needle and yarn
• decorations (fabric markers, beads, felt scraps, etc.)

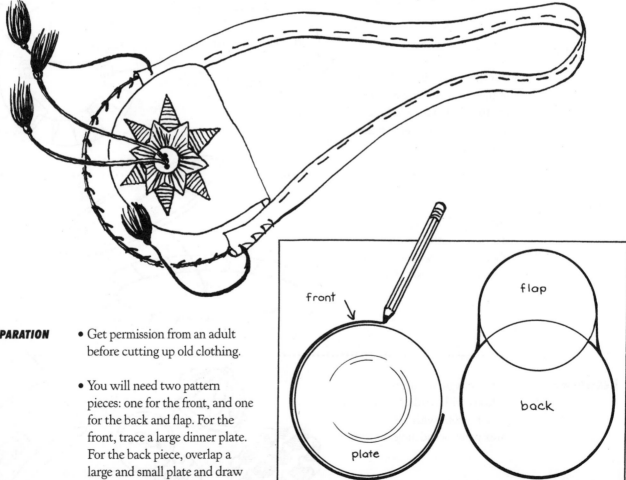

● **PREPARATION**
• Get permission from an adult before cutting up old clothing.

• You will need two pattern pieces: one for the front, and one for the back and flap. For the front, trace a large dinner plate. For the back piece, overlap a large and small plate and draw around them as shown.

- **INSTRUCTIONS**

1. Trace the paper pattern onto the material and cut it out.

2. Cut a strip about 75 cm by 8 cm for a shoulder strap.

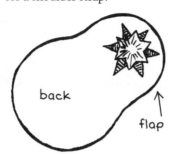

3. Decorate the flap of the bag with embroidery, beads, glued felt shapes or markers.

4. Sew the front to the back using the overcast stitch. Knot the ends securely. Trim off the top curved edge of the front piece, as shown.

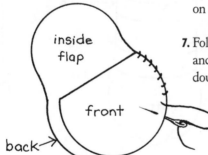

5. Add a button, ties or velcro to the flap to close the bag.

side view

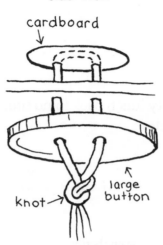

6. Fold one end of the strap in half around one side of the bag. Stitch through the bag to hold the strap firmly in place. Repeat with the other end of the strap on the other side.

7. Fold the rest of the strap in half and glue or sew it to keep it doubled over.

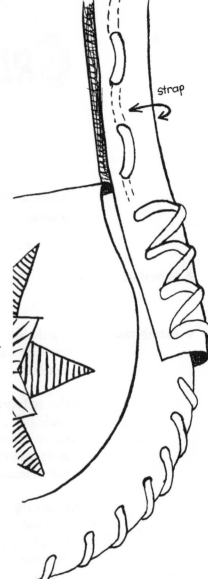

- **VARIATION**

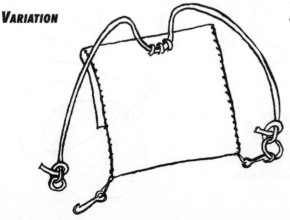

- Cut a rectangle three times as long as you want your finished backpack to be. Fold in thirds to form the front, back and flap. Stitch the side seams. Make straps from a 75-cm length of nylon rope. Wrap cut ends in tape or have an adult melt them.

- Use metal rings and clasps to attach straps at the bottom. Sew rope to back of the bag near the top. Sew through a piece of cardboard inside the backpack to make it stronger.

GRUB TUB

Make a nifty lunch pack in no time from a couple of plastic bottles.

● MATERIALS   • *2 large, clean, plastic pop bottles* • *scissors* • *metal paper fasteners* • *squeeze-on fabric paints*

● INSTRUCTIONS

1. Cut the bottom from one bottle, leaving about 1 cm of the narrower mid-section.

2. Cut the bottom from the second bottle, right at the top of the widest section. This should fit over the narrow part on the bottom section of your grub tub.

3. From the leftovers, cut a strip 1 cm wide and 22 cm long for the latch. Cut a 2 to 3 cm wide strip for the handle. Make the handle as long as you would like.

4. Punch a small hole in each end of the handle and the latch. Attach them to the bottom of your tub with metal paper fasteners, as shown.

5. Decorate your grub tub with squeeze-on fabric paints.

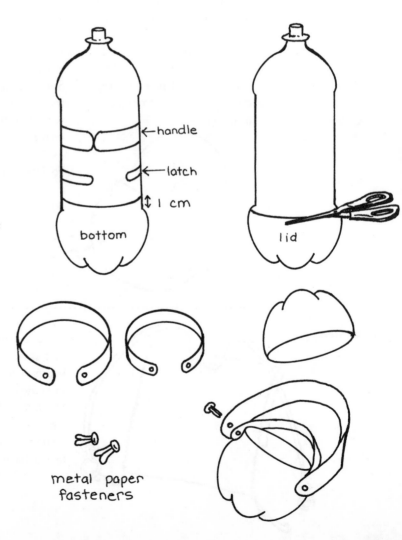

- **VARIATION**

- Make a rectangular grub tub from two large plastic oil or vinegar bottles. Cut out the pieces as shown.

box

- Slit the two back corners of the lid. Poke three holes in that edge. Attach the lid to the top of the box with metal paper fasteners to make a hinged lid.

- Poke a large hole in the latch of the lid. Close the lid and mark the hole on the box. Poke two small holes in the box, one on either side of the mark. Sew a bead, button or tie onto the box. Pop the bead through the hole to hold the lid closed.

- Use paper fasteners to attach a handle. Decorate as you like.

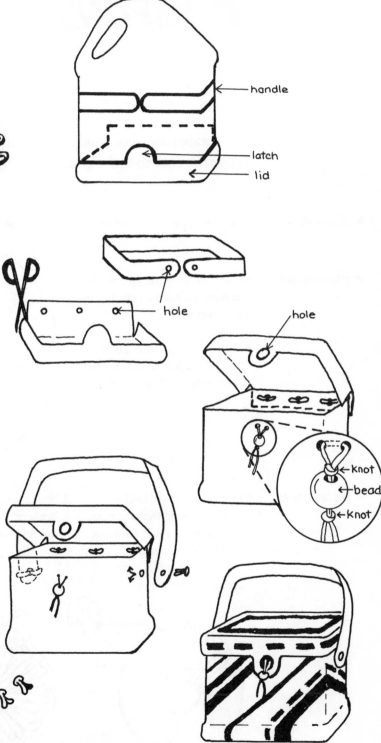

handle

latch

lid

hole

hole

knot

bead

knot

POMPONS

Decorate hats, shoes and everything in between with colorful, easy-to-make pompons.

- **MATERIALS**
  - yarn • scissors • cereal box or other thin cardboard

- **PREPARATION**
  - Cut two cardboard circles 10 cm in diameter with a 4 cm hole in the center of each.

  - Wind some yarn into a ball small enough to fit through the hole in the cardboard circles.

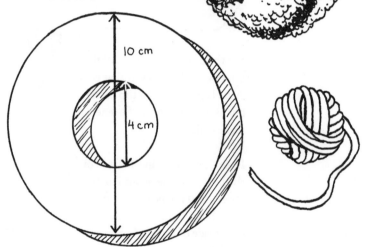

10 cm

4 cm

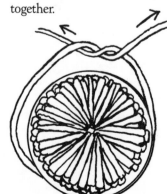

- **INSTRUCTIONS**

1. Put the cardboard circles together. Wind the yarn around the rim and through the hole over and over, completely covering the cardboard. Go around the circles four times.

2. Slide the point of the scissors between the two circles and carefully snip the yarn all around the edge.

3. Put a piece of yarn around the middle, between the two circles. Pull it tight and knot it several times to hold the strands of yarn together.

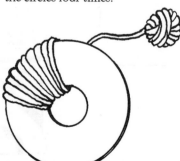

4. Slip the cardboard circles off, fluff the pompon and trim any uneven strands.

5. Attach pompons to hats, safety pins or hair elastics. Or make a large multi-colored pompon to use as a fun indoor ball.

• **VARIATION 1**

• Make your pompons into fuzzy critters by gluing on googly eyes and felt feet.

• **VARIATION 2**

• Try making these plump pompon birds. Make pompons as above, winding four layers of yarn in the color of the bird you want to make. Trim the finished pompon to the desired shape, and use fabric glue to add felt shapes for beaks, eyes, wings and so on.

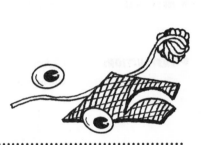

black and white felt

black felt

brown felt

beige pompom

chickadee

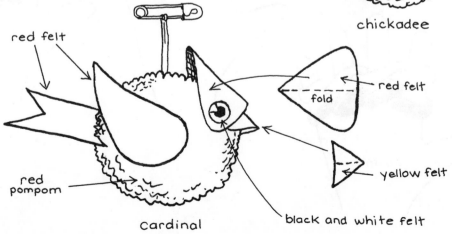

red felt

red felt

fold

red pompom

yellow felt

black and white felt

cardinal

• • • • • HEADBAND

Weave together pieces of old nylons or tights to make a colorful headband or neckrope.

● MATERIALS • old clean nylons, tights, stretchy socks or T-shirt sleeves • scissors

● INSTRUCTIONS

1. Cut circles 1 to 3 cm wide from the legs of the nylons.

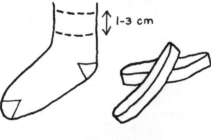

2. Twist a circle in and out around the four upright fingers of one hand. Twist a second circle onto your fingers on top of the first.

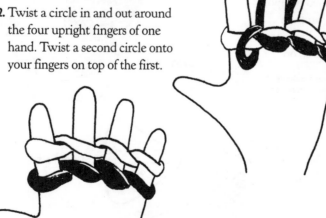

palm

3. Pick up the bottom loop at the back of your first finger. Lift it up and over your first finger.

4. Lift the loop on your second finger up and over your second finger the same way. Repeat for third and fourth fingers. The first circle should now be in the palm of your hand.

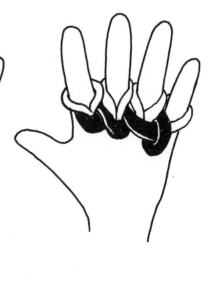

5. Twist another circle in and out around your four upright fingers. Lift the loops up and over as before. Repeat with more circles until your rope is as long as you like.

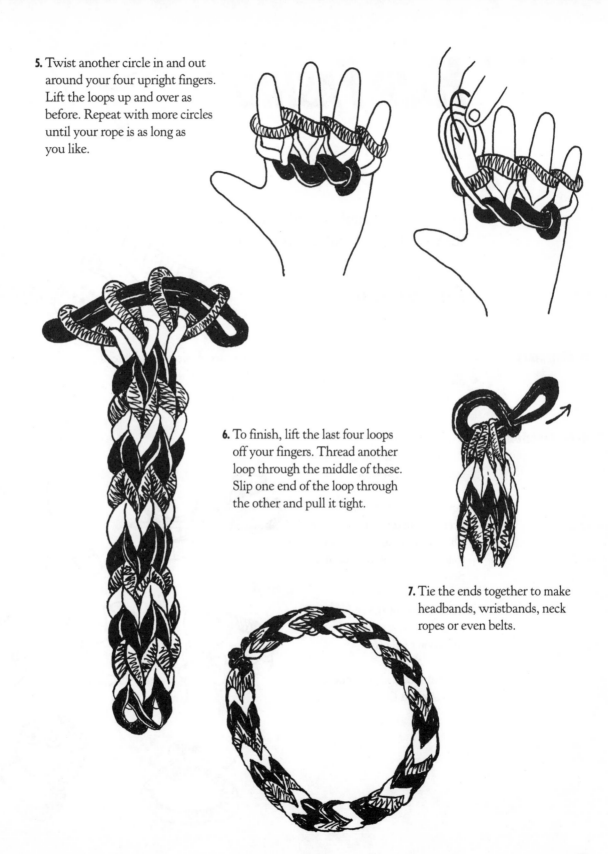

6. To finish, lift the last four loops off your fingers. Thread another loop through the middle of these. Slip one end of the loop through the other and pull it tight.

7. Tie the ends together to make headbands, wristbands, neck ropes or even belts.

HAIR FASHION

Old T-shirts, baubles, beads and ribbon can be turned into great stuff for your hair.

PONYTAIL HOLDERS

- **MATERIALS**
  - old T-shirts, sweatshirts, tights or nylons • scissors • needle and thread
  - decorations (buttons, beads, pompons, etc.)

- **INSTRUCTIONS**

  1. Cut nylons, tights, T-shirt sleeves or sweatshirt cuffs into circles 1 to 4 cm wide.

  2. Sew a button, pompon, beads or even a small toy onto each one. Or twist two different colors together and sew your decoration on.

  3. Be sure to knot the ends of the thread securely so your decorations don't fall off.

  4. Here are some ideas for decorating your hair ties.

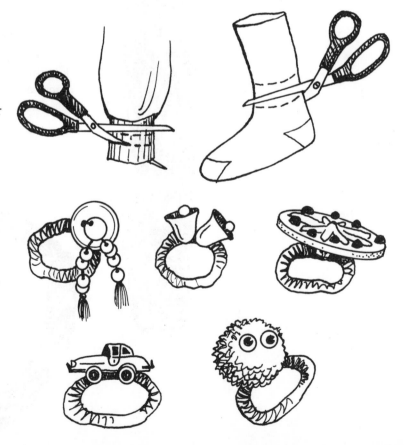

Ribbon Fashion

- **Materials**
  - *fine ribbon or yarn* • *scissors* • *darning needle*
  - *hair accessory (hairband, barrette, comb or bobby pin)*

- **Instructions**

  1. Tie one end of the ribbon securely to the hair accessory before you begin wrapping. Cover the knotted end of the ribbon as you wrap.

  2. To change colors, simply knot a new color on and cover the knot as you wind.

  3. When you finish wrapping, knot the end securely and use a large darning needle to pull the end back through the wrapped portion. Snip off the end.

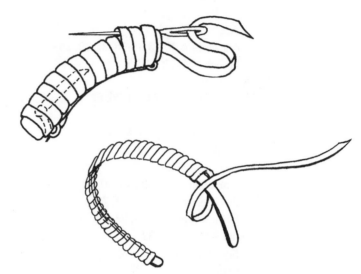

- **Variation**

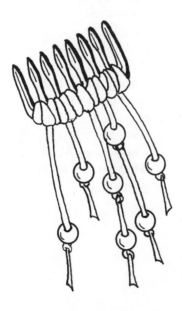

  - Tie extra bits of ribbon, yarn or thin strips of material onto a comb, barrette or bobby pin. Slip a bead on each ribbon and knot underneath to hold the bead in place. Or attach bits of curling ribbon. Pull each piece between your thumb and a dull knife several times to curl it.

INDEX